choosing
My
religion

choosing my religion

(r.c.) Sproul

BakerBooks
A Division of Baker Book House Co
Grand Rapids, Michigan 49516

Published by Baker Books
a division of Baker Book House Company
P.O. Box 6287, Grand Rapids, MI 49516-6287

Printed in the United States of America

Library of Congress Cataloging-in-Publication Data

Sproul, R.C. (Robert Charles), 1939–
Choosing my religion / R.C. Sproul.
p. cm.
ISBN 0-8010-5575-X (pbk.)
1. Apologetics. I. Title.
BT1102.S584 1996
239—dc20 95-45753

C O N T E N T S

one one one one one one one one

1

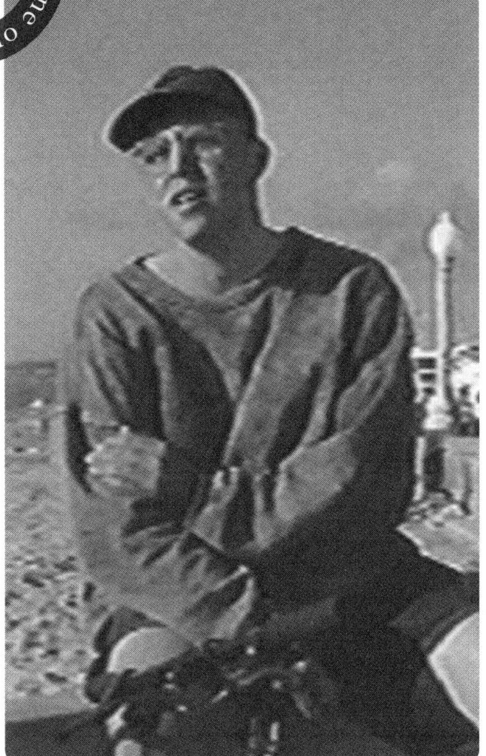

image is everything

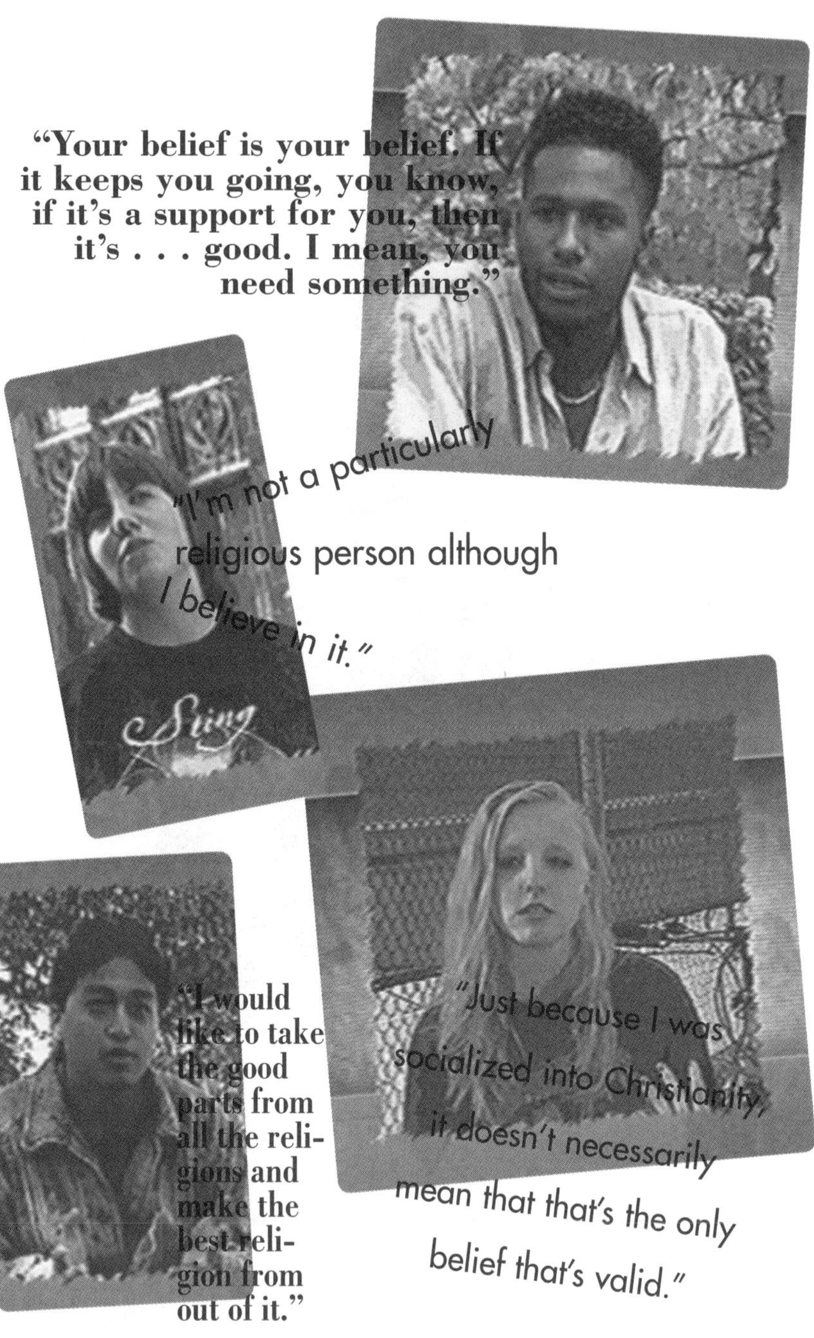
"Your belief is your belief. If it keeps you going, you know, if it's a support for you, then it's . . . good. I mean, you need something."
"I'm not a particularly religious person although I believe in it."
"I would like to take the good parts from all the religions and make the best religion from out of it."
"Just because I was socialized into Christianity, it doesn't necessarily mean that that's the only belief that's valid."

"I think Buddhists can go to heaven, just as well as Christians."
"I haven't come across any real religions that were contradictory, except for maybe Satanism or something like that."
"In any religion that doesn't deal with Jesus Christ as their Savior, people are not going to go to heaven."
"I believe in reincarnation. I figure if you live your life the right way you'll come back the right way. You live your life the wrong way, you'll come back the wrong way."

THE STUDENTS WHO made these statements are struggling to make a decision about truth. Is there one real truth? Does truth matter, or is everything relative?

Let me begin to suggest an answer to those questions by inviting you to participate in a quiz. There are two questions. To make things interesting, let's imagine that if you answer either question correctly you will win a Mitsubishi Eclipse (4-cylinder, 140 hp, with CD deck and a sun roof? Hey, why not?).

The first question is simple: A large glass jar filled with jelly beans sits on the table before you. *How many pieces of candy are in the jar?*

I wonder if that physics lesson on mass and displacement would be of help here. Probably not. Finally all contestants have written down their answers. Ready for question 2:

What is the best flavor of ice cream?

Where is Baskin-Robbins when you need them? You mean which flavor is the most popular? Which flavor sells best?

Simply name the *best* flavor.

All answers written down?

How many jelly beans are in the jar? One guess comes in at 250, another at 500, and another at 643. One joker has guessed there are 55,732—and one-half. Your guess was 412. The actual number of beans: 413.

All right! . . . Just toss over those ignition keys!

No can do. No one guessed correctly. There was an actual number of beans in the jar, and you did not come up with that number. Close doesn't count.

Maybe someone did better on the second question. Answers are varied: Strawberry swirl. Mackinac Island Fudge. The ever-popular vanilla. Neopolitan.

Isn't Neopolitan three flavors?

Oh, that's from the guy with the 55,000-plus jelly beans.

The correct answer is: There is no correct answer. The *best* flavor of ice cream is the flavor you personally prefer. It is really just a matter of personal preference or the flavor you associate in your mind with pleasant memories, the one you shared with that cute sophomore and which now gives you warm fuzzies when you think of it.

TYING THE MIND UP IN KNOTS

There once was a Roman government bureaucrat named Pontius Pilate who preferred *favorite flavor of ice cream truth* to *number of jelly beans total truth*. One day he was hearing the case of a most unlikely criminal defendant named Jesus Christ—a defendant who claimed to have *the* truth (John 18:38).

"What is truth?" Pilate asked.

We don't know if Pilate sneered when he said those words. The Bible doesn't tell us about his tone of voice. But if Pilate did scorn the idea of absolute truth he would feel right at home in today's world. Absolute truth—the number of jelly beans in the jar—presents a narrow, constricting view of reality. How much better if truth is in the eye of the beholder, the comfortably relative image truth of personal preference. Relative truth is based on an image. A personal truth doesn't discount other, equally engaging truths. I am free to follow my truth. You are free to follow yours.

This way of looking at truth is called "relativism." According to this philosophy, all truth is relative. What's true for you need not be true for anyone else and cannot be true for everyone else. Nothing—absolutely nothing—is true for everyone. One atheist philosopher summed up this view when he said, "There can be no eternal truth since there is no divine mind to think it."

But wait a second. To say that absolutely nothing is absolutely true is to affirm absolute truth. If that argument is true, then it is automatically false. Either way it is wrong. And to say that there can be no eternal truth is to claim that there is the eternal truth that there is no eternal truth. Such statements are self-contradictory and absurd.

Would you base your life on the belief that all statements are false? I suspect you would doubt the sanity of anyone who seriously asked you to do so. A philosophy that denies the possibility of truth is a philosophy that denies its own truth-claims. No one should take it seriously.

The subject of this book—choosing a religion—is based on the premise that there is, among all the possible avenues of relative truth, a path of uniquely, absolutely true truth.

If there is no such path, we live in a relative universe, and all is utter nonsense.

KNOWING *MATTERS*

Every man and woman at some time in life comes to the point of turning toward one truth to the exclusion of all competing truths. Before us lie all options of beliefs on which we may base our lives. The fact that we all make this choice (and choosing not to choose is a choice) is one indication that there is a correct path somewhere. There is one existential reality, and you and I are part of that reality. It exists and holds things together. No reality we can comprehend exists in a totally contradictory universe, with no absolute truths. Even Isaac Asimov could not turn such a universe into a science fiction novel. Its reality would change from page to page. Fortunately, even the relativist makes assumptions based on a shared, consistent reality in which certain truths are true.

That doesn't mean the system you choose must be consistent, logical, or even rational. It can tie your mind up in knots. But you must choose, and that choice will be your religion. You will come to complete the sentence: "I believe in. . . ." You may come to rechoose later, and affirm: "I used to believe in . . . , but now I believe in. . . ." At each point you will believe in something, and that belief will shape your loves, hates, ideals, behavior, and goals. Your life's pattern, and most of its choices, will be determined in that moment you complete the sentence: "I believe in. . . ."

The statements at the beginning of this chapter were made by students who are in the process of choosing a religion. There are as many definitions of the word "religion" as there are perspectives of theology, psychology, sociology, and anthropology. But let me suggest one that will give us a point of reference: A religion is a life-defining system of believed truths. Stated another way: Religion is how I complete the sentence: "I believe in. . . ."

It is profoundly sad, even terrifying, that the fashionable religion is based on relativism—a negating of reality that completes the sentence this way: "I believe in *no truth*."

TRUTH AND REALITY

In the early 1990s the United States went through one of its most vicious, embarrassing moments in their history involving a question of truth: A man was nominated by the president to be a justice on the United States Supreme Court, the highest court in this land.

He had to be approved by the U.S. Senate. As he was questioned, a woman who had once worked for him came forward to charge that he had sexually harassed her.

Anita Hill had become a law professor in the years since she had worked for Clarence Thomas. Law professors are considered to be rational observers, painstakingly meticulous in dealing with facts. We would assume that they are truthful. Her story sounded credible.

Judge Thomas had a distinguished record on the bench and his reputation for fairness and integrity had elevated him to the point where he was singled out for one of the nation's most important jobs. And, point by point, Thomas denied doing or saying the things Anita Hill charged. His account of the facts did not align with hers beyond the fact that she had worked for him. He would not even concede that something he did or said might have been misinterpreted. She charged that he had pressured her for sexual favors. To each supposed statement she said he had made, Judge Thomas responded with force: "I never said that."

Over the course of the Senate hearing all kinds of people appeared before the senators and television cameras. Some people said, "Anita Hill never tells lies like this." Another group said, "Clarence Thomas never tells lies like this." How could anybody determine with certainty who was telling the truth? I watched the proceedings on television, and I didn't know.

The amazing reaction, though, came from the United States senators, whose opinions were the ones that really counted. Some senators had obvious political interests in choosing one side over another, so their findings weren't surprising. Others appeared before television cameras, though, and announced: "Well, you know, I think they're both telling the truth."

I didn't know who was telling the truth, but one thing I knew for sure: It was impossible that both of them were telling the truth. This was a question about reality, about what *really* happened, not about what Clarence Thomas or Anita Hill was feeling. The issue was: Did this man say these things, or didn't he? If he said them, he couldn't at the same time have not said them. If he didn't say them, it couldn't be true, could it, that he did say them?

We have established law courts and a judicial system of trial on the premise that there is one uniquely true truth among various conflicting accounts. A defendant charged with murder is asked: "Did you, on the night of February 13, 1991, with malice of forethought, stab this woman in the throat?" The defendant pleads "Not guilty." No, he didn't do it, so that is not a statement of the reality of what happened on that night. The court convenes, the evidence is brought forth, and the jury evaluates it, trying to get at the one truth, for only one truth is possible.

A religion of no truth means we store our brains in the same jar with the senators who decided Clarence Thomas and Anita Hill were both telling the truth. It is just as logical to take a look at the jar of jelly beans and say, "There is no one correct answer here. I can believe there are 412 pieces of candy, and you can believe there are 55,732.5, and we can both be right. It really doesn't matter, after all. What counts is our preferred image of reality." Yet image works for choosing a favorite flavor of ice cream. It doesn't work when an objective reality exists—the correct number of 413 jelly beans.

What process of logic do the following students use as they complete the sentence, "I believe in . . ."?

> "If two people came together, and one person said that there is a God, and one person said there isn't a God, they could both be right at the same time, because it's all just opinion of what you believe and what you were brought up to believe."
>
> "When it comes to everybody giving different opinions of God and what he looks like and all that, everybody has their own opinion of God. When you get to know God, he's whoever you want him to be. He could be that tree. Well, God's a tree today."
>
> "I like to respect all religions the same. Just because I was socialized into Christianity doesn't necessarily mean that's the only belief that's valid."
>
> "People can find happiness through Jesus or through Hare Krishna or whichever form they see God in."
>
> "Basically, if you read the Qur'an or the Bible, they're a majority of the same thing, but there's only a little bit of difference, like in name and things like that."
>
> "Muslims refer to God as Allah; Jamaicans refer to God as Jah; Christians refer to God as Jesus; but I guess it's just a spiritual form, because there's many names for him."
>
> "I guess God exists for some people and for some people he doesn't."

Try similar reasoning to justify an answer that has been marked wrong on a mathematics quiz: "Teacher, you are unfair. This answer may be wrong for you, but it's right for me. In fact, I believe wholeheartedly that 2 + 2 = 5, so for me it's true that 2 + 2 = 5."

I don't think so.

The correct answer is correct, and an incorrect answer is incorrect, whether you believe it or not. That is just the way things are, and wishful thinking won't change the relationships among numbers. Some perverse society might decide to take a poll. Computing the results, they find that 78 percent of the people believe that 2 + 2 = 5, 20 percent believe that 2 + 2 = 4, and 2 percent are undecided. Based on those results, a law is passed decreeing that 2 + 2 = 5, and that it is an offense against the common good to use any other version of mathematics. Does this law change the facts?

No, the actual truth is true, even if not one person anywhere believes it is true. Anyone who builds a house in a society of relative truth would have a choice: Break the popular law and come up with an accurate measurement, or break the law of reality and come up with walls that don't meet.

Apply the logic of relativism to basic assumptions about God and behavior. A majority of people in our society have contracted a mental computer virus in the logic circuits. It is triggered by any invitation to theological or ethical reasoning. Suddenly the person's mental defenses against self-contradictory reasoning are overridden by a message that flashes on and off:

"All is relative—*beep.*

"All is relative—*beep.*

"All is relative—*beep. . . .*"

Here's how it works. Ask someone, "Is it good for a person to have an abortion for convenience?"

"Well, it's not right for me. I wouldn't do it. But it's okay for other people if they choose to do it. If that's what they want to do, then it's okay for them."

Translation: Choosing whether to abort an unborn baby is the same as choosing a best flavor of ice cream.

TRUTH AND AUTHORITY

If an objective reality stands behind life, that reality defines the way the world functions. Attempts to bypass this reality should carry the surgeon general's warning: "Ignoring truth is hazardous to your life and sanity." I do not want to drive across a bridge designed by an engineer who believed the numbers in structural stress models are relative truths. Things follow rules, or an authority structure. Chemical elements do not change the way they interact without good reason. Program a computer with the equations to account for variables it will encounter, and the computer will tick off astoundingly complex formulations with minute accuracy. It works because we can trust in the absolute authority of the laws governing reality.

Absolute truth, then, empowers us. Once we learn what the truth is as well as its structure of authority, we can move out confidently, trusting in the authority structure that governs life. Functioning in a world without absolute truth and the authority behind it would be a hideous experience. We could trust nothing.

Remember the philosopher who said, "There can be no eternal truth since there is no divine mind to think it." I'm not sure how this individual would define "eternal truth," but anyone who has really thought about it can come up with a number of truths that show every indication of being eternal, systemic, and absolute. That brings into serious question the second half of his equation—that there is no divine mind to think eternal truths. I would not care to defend this proposition.

Could it be that people aren't really bothered by absolutes after all? Perhaps the bothersome thing is that they indicate the existence of an absolute Authority. An absolute Authority calls for submission. Worse, it demands that I submit. Check for the different feelings about authority in the following statements by students who were asked where they have found their personal standards for moral living:

"Basically, if I don't like it then it's wrong, and if I like it then it's right. Simple as that."

"Basically, from experiences, from what I see, read, feel, basically just what feels right for me. There's no particular thing that makes me say, 'This is morally right or this is morally wrong.' "

"I'm always consistent with what I'm sure is right, but whether or not the Man upstairs perceives it as being right, that's another story."

"My standard for faith and belief comes from the Bible. I believe the Bible to be without error, perfect, the living, God-breathed Word of God. And through those Scriptures is where I obtain my guidelines, my morals, with the way Jesus Christ has told me to live my life."

"The Bible doesn't have much authority over my life, I basically go on my own and I have my own certain morals."

"Whether something's right or wrong, I mean that's very individual. I think that it all depends on circumstances of your life, et cetera, et cetera. I decide whether something's wrong for me, you know. If it's not morally correct for me or something like that, then I won't do it—if something's good for me, if it's going to make me happy, or if it's going to get me what I want, et cetera."

"Morals are morals. Everyone has their own."

I'm not certain what the person who made the latter statement means, but the statement is correct. Morals are universal. Everyone has a set. No archaeologist has ever found evidence for the existence of a truly "amoral" society. Only someone who has fully crossed the threshold into insanity lives without some moral authority structure. The students who say they follow their own preferred rights and wrongs are saying that they have subconsciously come to judge some actions and experiences to have higher value then other actions and experiences. We call our moral standards "value judgments." The relativist has them, just as much as does the Christian or the Buddhist. The only difference is the location of the authority base that holds up the value judgments.

One student quoted above found a single source for authority in the Bible. The assumption of this individual is that the Bible accurately conveys the thoughts and desires of the God who defines all ultimate truth. People may fear or discount that kind of revealed authority, but I certainly don't. If that view is accurate, I believe we are very fortunate to have an objective, exact, unchanging measure by which to define absolutes and make value judgments.

Far from being just one among many religions that makes such a claim, only the Judeo-Christian concept of God and revealed authority allows us such good fortune. Only Judeo-Christian belief claims that there exists a comprehensive revelation by which God addresses us directly and with authority. Not even Islam's Qur'an makes such a direct and personal claim to us in the name of the God who made the universe. Islamic Scripture is divine revelation only in the Arabic language communicated by vision to Muhammad—and that was communicated by angels and not God. The Qur'an offers vague guidelines and principles as well. To establish comprehensive principles for living, orthodox Muslims turn to the Hadith, a collection of traditions gathered by holy men that makes no pretense of being divinely revealed. And this is as close to the truth-claims made by Christianity and orthodox Judaism as any other religion gets.

AUTHORITATIVE IMAGE

Most people use personal preference as their authority. This is set out eloquently by another of the students quoted above:

> "If it's not morally correct for me or something like that, then I won't do it—if something's good for me, if it's going to make me happy or if it's going to get me what I want, et cetera, then . . ."

"Yes, I can have a solidly relative authority," this person might assert. "I deem that something is valuable, and therefore moral, if

1. it's good for me.
2. it makes me happy.
3. it gets me what I want."

Others use very similar criteria:

"It feels right."

Or,

> "I basically go on my own" (this person is in the improv theatre school of life).

All these criteria look to image—subjective feelings of value. All this subjective analysis of life may not be as liberated as it appears. Parents, peers, society, mood, health, and even indigestion from eating pizza with anchovies all influence subjective feelings. But there is an assumption that we can call the shots: "I believe this action in this situation has value. Doing something else wouldn't be as 'good.' "

Think about this for a minute. If my feelings call the moral shots, and there truly is no absolute truth to worry about, what possible difference does it make what my subjective feelings tell me to do? It may feel right to help a little old lady across the street or it may feel right to mug her and cut her throat. If there is no absolute standard, then saying an action "feels right" makes as much sense as saying something "feels yellow."

But wait. Let's be fair to the guy who set out three perfectly good criteria for moral action. An action is good if it (1) is good for me, (2) makes me happy, and (3) gets me what I want.

Let's try it out. Question: Is it morally right to cheat on an exam?

Flunking a class will not do my happiness level any good at all. Cheating will help me pass, which should contribute to getting me what

I want. Therefore, cheating on tests is a moral good.

However, cheating on tests is not a moral good for the person sitting next to me. His cheating may raise the grade curve and lower my grade, which will not make me happy. Also, this student plans to go to medical school and may one day be my doctor. I want my doctor to be well prepared to diagnose and treat me. Therefore, cheating is a moral good for me, but a moral evil for my future doctor.

Of course, cheating is only a moral good if I get away with it. I certainly won't be happy if I am kicked out of school. And I also need to be prepared for whatever job I end up with, or I will lose it, which won't contribute to my happiness or get me what I want. All told, passing a course by cheating is a small thing to be happy about in the big scheme of things. I might be cheating myself out of the happiness I would have had if I had mastered the material and been able to use the knowledge I gained later.

Therefore, maybe cheating isn't so morally right.

I'm so confused.

Subjective values can be confusing. Who can know? What seems right may in fact turn out very wrong. Sorting out all possible consequences can take more time than studying to pass without cheating.

Let's take another example: You are desperately in love with the hunk quarterback on the football team. And, joy of joys, he likewise expresses eternal devotion to you. He says that people who feel this way toward one another must not hold back anything. You must give yourself to him, body and soul. He seems to be more focused on the body gift. Having that satisfying physical relationship with you will inspire him to play as he has never played before come Saturday.

Obviously this jock has settled in *his* mind what will be oh-so-good for him, make him happy, and get him what he wants. What about you? Being the object of the desire of this MVP makes you feel good about yourself. Having him at your side will transform your social standing. That will make you happy, as will the prospects of having a hunk husband. He's bound to do great things in life, which should give you materially what you want. For starters, what you want is to be valued as a person, to have someone who cares for you.

Is something wrong with this picture?

It feels good. It looks good.

But your feelings are sadly uninformed about the testosterone at work in the body of your hero. This guy may like you as a person, but the fact that he wants you sexually has nothing to do with how he values your personhood. Giving in to his demands will lower your value in his eyes. The chances of marriage growing from freely given sex are dim. If marriage does occur, counselors are very pessimistic about the lifelong success of such a relationship. Also be aware that the high school and college all-conference star often does not stand out in the professional world. Your dreams of a comfortable future are not founded on solid evidence.

This is to say nothing of the possibilities of contracting a sexually transmitted disease or becoming pregnant.

The ramifications go on and on. If your authority is feelings, thinking through potential consequences may keep you from making a mistake, but I wouldn't bet on it. More likely you won't remember half of those possible consequences in the heat of a passionate moment. The tendency, at least, is to apply all the warnings and personal common sense to other people. They might get caught. I won't. My situation is different. He wouldn't dump me like that other guy dumped her.

I fear for anyone with such standards:

> "There are things that are just intuitive. You have to make a balance because whenever you make a decision you're not going to have an absolute right, or an absolute wrong either. You have to balance it yourself. If there were a way of coming up with an absolute right I'm sure I'd be taking a course right now at school on how to figure out what it was."
>
> "I see everything as relative. The way I should treat somebody might not be how somebody else should treat somebody."
>
> "I can say what's true for me, and I'm sure everyone can say what's true for themselves. But I have no idea what's true for everyone."
>
> "I think that it depends on the person who's looking at the situation. I don't think there's an absolute standard of right and wrong."

THE MYTH OF RELATIVE TRUTH

Relative truth simply does not work as a guide, but even if it did, that is not the whole story. The more profound question is whether relative truth is true. If you think for five minutes about what these people are basing their beliefs on, you will be driven to the conclusion that it is all smoke. It can't possibly be true. On a college campus I was debating with a young woman the question: "Does God exist?" She finally turned to me and asked, "Well, Professor Sproul, do you find religion meaningful?"

"Yes."

"Do you pray to God?"

"Yes."

"Do you like to sing hymns?"

"Yes."

"Do you go to church on Sunday morning?"

"Yes."

"Do you engage in fellowship activities?"

"Yes."

"Well then, since this is all so wonderful and meaningful for you, then for you God exists. But that's irrelevant to me and to my life. I don't find any meaning whatsoever in praying or going to church or in singing hymns or doing any of that religious stuff. So for me, there is no God."

I was honestly confused by her reasoning.

"I'm not talking about my religious experience or your religious experience. We're discussing the question of whether in reality there is such a being whom we call God. If God does not exist in reality, all my praying, all my singing, all my preaching, all my church-going activities, all of that stuff won't have the power to conjure him up. I can't create him. If he does exist apart from me and apart from you, all of your unbelief, all of your disinterest, does not have the power to kill him."

For the Ligonier Ministries video series "Choosing My Religion," team members wandered around college campuses with a video camera, doing spontaneous interviews. It's really not hard to get people to talk in front of a camera. We heard one student after another saying, "Well, God is whatever you want him to be." "All religions are equally valid. All religions are equally true. If your religion is Buddhism and yours is Confucianism and yours is Judaism and yours is Islam and yours is Christianity, they're all the same; they all believe in the same God and they're all true."

But, again, this is impossible. All religions are obviously not equally true, because they don't believe the same things. They believe contradictory things. Christianity believes that Jesus was God incarnate. Other world religions say Jesus was a nice guy, a great teacher, a man of principle, but certainly not God. Jesus is either God, or he is not; he cannot be divine and not divine at the same time and in the same relationship.

"I don't really think Jesus is God because they are . . . I guess they are kind of the same. They have the same beliefs. But I don't know if you could characterize them as the same person."

"Jesus was just a normal human being at that time who could perform miracles."

"I can believe that Jesus is the divine Son of God. I do believe that's true."

"Jesus was supposedly God's Son that came down to earth to save everyone and forgive their sins. What role do I think he played? I don't think he played any role because I don't think he existed."

Somebody is wrong about Jesus. I believe that he is God, and either I'm wrong or Muhammad was wrong. If Jesus is God, then Muhammad was wrong. The truth-claims of Christians and Muslims cannot both be true. It might be more pleasant if all religions could be equally true. We would not be divided over religious questions. But because there can be only one truth, and I am utterly certain of what that truth is, I cannot keep from telling other people—and arguing with them occasionally. While there are those who simply enjoy arguing, most people who defend their religion do so because they care passionately about ultimate truth. We understand that truth matters and that ultimate truth makes all the difference in a person's life.

THE SEARCH FOR TRUTH BEGINS

Has an idea ever changed your life? Have you ever encountered a reality so powerful, so cataclysmic, that you could never be the same afterwards? In 1952 my life changed forever when I fell in love. I was thirteen at the time, and I had to put up with snide comments about "puppy love." But I knew I had encountered a special person, and my life wasn't the same. Ten years later I married that person, and forty years later she's the last person I see when I go to bed at night and the first person I see when I get up.

But a more catalytic moment came on September 13, 1957, when I encountered Christ and came to understand that this Person is real and that he plays for keeps.

My life changed. Was I deluded? Did I deceive myself by some kind of religious experience into thinking that I had encountered truth when in fact it was imagination? That's a theoretical possibility. But it matters to me whether God is true and real. When someone says that Christ can be both real and imaginary, both true and false, depending on my feelings, I want to respond, "Wake up. Put your brains back in your head." He can't possibly be both.

We who live in late-twentieth-century America have embraced relativism and go to ridiculous lengths to apply it to religion. It is hard to believe that millions of intelligent human beings are running around saying all religions are equally true. We all know better.

In part our self-deception is virtuous: We believe that everybody should be treated equally and should be free to express whatever religion they believe. The government has no business sticking a rifle in your face and saying, "You have to be a Christian." Christianity, in fact, calls me to love people regardless of their religion. I am to treat them kindly, and to ensure their justice.

But that is not the same as saying they are right. The law gives us a legal right to be theologically wrong. Nobody will throw you in jail or increase your taxes if you make a mistake about God. God, however, cares about truth. He never gives you the right to be wrong—particularly to be wrong about him.

But should people who believe in relative truth care about what God thinks, or believe that there is a God who thinks at all? On our travels around American college campuses almost everyone we talked to said they believe in God. A typical response might be: "Sure. I believe in some kind of higher power, some kind of being."

The real issue for most of us is not whether there is a God. We know there is. The issue is: Who is God? Above all, our search to finish the sentence, "I believe in . . ." must be framed around another question: What is God really like?

We will look for an answer to that question by asking another question that is almost as difficult to answer: What am I really like?

two two two two two two two two

II

the ultimate spring break

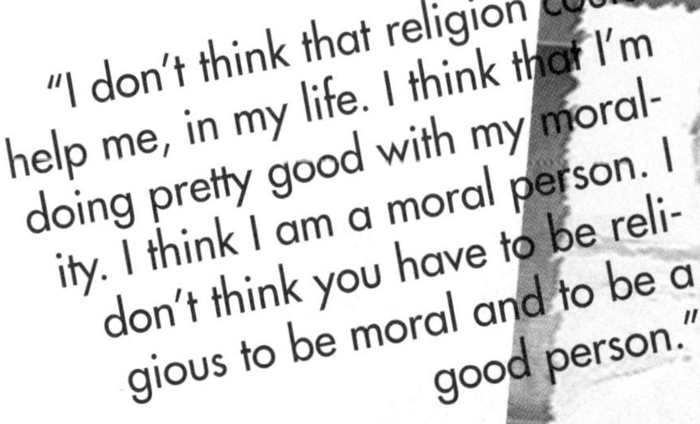

"I don't think that religion could help me, in my life. I think that I'm doing pretty good with my morality. I think I am a moral person. I don't think you have to be religious to be moral and to be a good person."

"People, a lot of times, put a lot of religion into values and stuff, and I just don't think that that's right."

"When it comes to a moral decision, it's not if it's right or wrong or something. I pretty much check whether it's illegal or not."

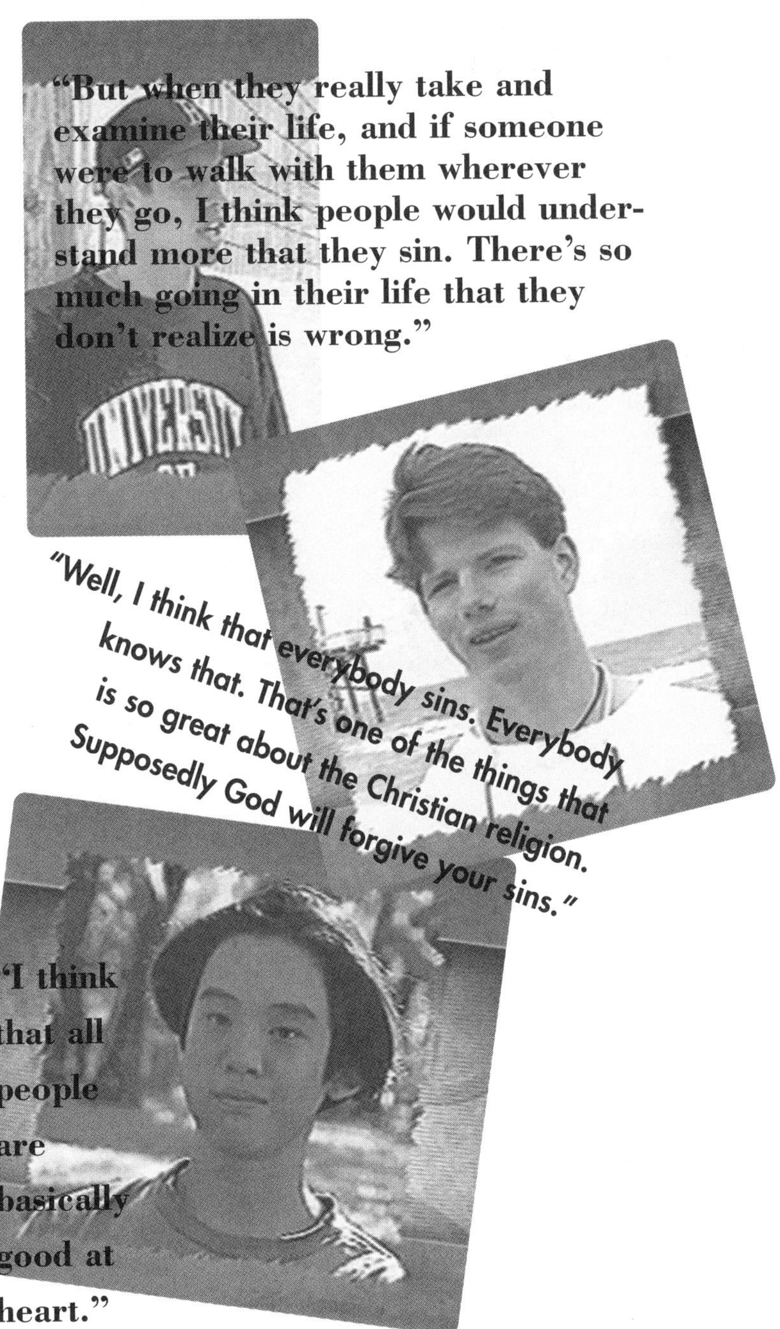
"But when they really take and examine their life, and if someone were to walk with them wherever they go, I think people would understand more that they sin. There's so much going in their life that they don't realize is wrong."
"Well, I think that everybody sins. Everybody knows that. That's one of the things that is so great about the Christian religion. Supposedly God will forgive your sins."
"I think that all people are basically good at heart."

WE ARE LOOKING for truth about God. Who is God? What is God like? Can we find a religion that is built on absolute truth? Where can we go for research on a term paper like that?

Let's begin at Daytona Beach, Florida.

God has a condo there?

No, but Jesus Christ told a story about God and Daytona Beach. Or it would have been about Daytona Beach if he had been talking to American college students.

His updated version would go something like this:

A man with two sons had been fairly successful in life, and as his boys finished high school they went on to the local university. The rule was that they would work in the family business as their class load permitted and that they would study hard so they could make something of themselves. In return, they were furnished with great food, a beautiful home, and their share, ultimately, of the family business.

THE FAR COUNTRY

Son number one dug right in and tried his best to make Dad proud. The trouble came after son number two drifted through high school and made it, barely, into college. Long about late February he took his father aside to make a business proposition.

"Dad, I know you've been working all your life and have a savings account and investments. I know you've written a will, so that when you die I'll inherit half of your fortune. Pop, I don't want to sit around hoping you die. That just wouldn't be right. Let's make a deal. How about letting me have my inheritance now?"

The father certainly had some misgivings, but he eventually agreed to the plan. He liquidated some assets and handed the son all the money in his share of the family estate. What do you suppose the son did after he received the inheritance? As soon as spring break came at the college he left, headed south for Daytona Beach.

Even if you haven't read the story Jesus told of the prodigal son in Luke 15 you likely have some idea about what happened next—especially if you've been in Daytona Beach at spring break. Cut loose from all the strings and rules, and with plenty of money burning his pocket, this guy financed the break bash of all time. He hit town in a Ferrari, checked into a luxurious suite, laid out a stash and booze, and gathered in the friends. After partying all night he crashed on the beach all day, then cruised to find an even better date for the next round.

After a week of the good life, he was starting to show some wear. His nerves were frazzled and he felt sick from the drugs and booze. He had the sunburn of his life. His unlimited bankroll had somehow vanished, and so had the Ferrari. If only he could remember what had happened to that car. His friends trashed the hotel room, he didn't have enough money to pay damages, and he was arrested for shoplifting something to eat. Things had gone from so good to so bad so quickly.

He was ashamed to go back home, and no one wanted to hire a leftover kid after the wave of young humanity had washed northward. He was out on the streets, now making friends with winos and pushers. He was not the man of the world he had thought. He was scared, and he was tired, and he was hungry. He just wanted to go home.

Finally, he had had enough. Father had every right to kick him out on his ear. But maybe Dad would give him a minimum wage job, or at least let him work for a place to sleep in the corner of the garage. So he slowly thumbed his way northward. Finally he was on familiar ground, dirty and stinking, but approaching the old home place.

Suddenly a figure burst from the doorway of his home. His father had seen him coming and ran down to the street to embrace him. After a bath he was treated to an enormous meal and assured that he would always have a place in the family. For the one who had been lost was again found.

SPRING BREAK IN A GARDEN

According to the Bible, that action illustrates what happened to the very first spring breakers, Adam and Eve, who lived in an unbelievably beautiful home—the Garden of Eden—but wanted to kick out of the boundaries and have some "fun." You may accept evolutionary ancestors, but I see a whole lot more reasons to believe the account told in Genesis 2 and 3, at the very beginning of the Bible. It has the ring of truth. The facts of life on earth perfectly fit the scenario described in Genesis and the rest of the Bible. Jesus' story about the lost son describes Adam and Eve and every human being's life since that fateful day when humans first rebelled against God. This story also tells us a little about the person who is in reality God.

What about this young man? He had been living at home with his father, enjoying whatever benefits his father had provided through all of the years of his life. While the father was providing these benefits the son had a relationship with his father. He lived every day in his father's presence.

This is precisely the relationship between the first people and God. God made them, put Adam and Eve in the garden, gave them all the benefits of a perfect society, gave them wonderful provisions. Of all of the trees in the garden God said to Adam and Eve, "You may freely eat." And in some personal fellowship that we cannot now imagine, God's presence entered the garden in the cool of the day, and Adam and Eve rushed to delight themselves in his nearness.

But one day they left. They decided, apparently, that what they really wanted were the benefits of God, but not him.

LOVING THE GIFTS OR THE GIVER?

That picture of selfishness is what we are like, too. The son said to his father, "Thank you very much for the inheritance. I appreciate the benefits. I'm out of here." He wanted his father's money; he did not want his father. I wonder how many people who say they love God *really* love God. It's *easy* to love God for the benefits he gives to us. In fact, I think most of us think we really ought to have those benefits, and it is only right that we get them.

But we don't really begin to love God until we love God for who he is. The Creator of the stunningly crafted universe is obviously, worth getting to know, and worth adoring for who he is rather than what he can give us. The root of Adam and Eve's fall was that they wanted their full inheritance before they were ready to receive it. They loved the goodies God gave them, and they thought they deserved more now, not later.

People today are the same, for the entire human race received an inheritance of selfishness and rebellion against God. The religion you choose may or may not have a god with whom to communicate. Most secularists have no trouble here, for they only have to talk to themselves. There are not many true atheists, for every heart cries out for a God. In fact, the Bible says that every person knows down deep inside that there is a God—even the agnostic who takes such pride in not knowing. Most people who take an active position against God actually want to see themselves as the center of the universe. They want to *be* God and have the ultimate authority over their own lives. If God is me, then communication with God is no big problem. Only the nihilist stands truly alone, shouting profanity into the wind. The nihilist glories in hopelessness, trying to kill whatever God-consciousness remains deep inside. I can imagine no hell as lonely as the world this poor fool attempts to build.

I said in chapter 1 that Christianity stands unique among the religions of the world. We have come to yet another place to view a unique quality of the God of the Christian. The Christian God is without bounds as maker of everything that is, and yet he still seeks to know and be known. He seeks fellowship. Allah stands cold and aloof from the worshiper of Islam. There can be worship directed to Allah, but no interpersonal communication. He is "other" from the creature. To an extent orthodox Jews look to an interpersonal God, as he is revealed in the Old Testament. They have a God with whom they can seek fellowship. There still is a difference between God as viewed by Judaism and God as viewed by Christianity. The God with whom I fellowship has gone to an unimaginable length to restore the communication that was lost in the rebellion of Adam and Eve. More about that later.

For the moment let's say you choose Christianity or Judaism, through which you are invited to approach God through the medium known as prayer. What's your prayer life like, if you have one? I'll tell you what the prayers of many

Christians are like. They who are invited to meet God and tell him they love him often pray like this:

> "Dear God. Please bless Mama, Daddy, Grandma, Uncle Fred, Aunt Sally . . . and now about what I need: Let me win the game, and get a new car. Let me have a date with Rachel on Friday, and. . . ."

In other words, we go to him with requests for benefits. "Give me my inheritance now." When he gives you a blessing you say, "Thank you very much," and you take off for Daytona Beach. And then you wonder why your faith doesn't keep you out of trouble once you get there.

The first thing the prodigal son does in Jesus' story is to leave his father's house. Did he then rent an apartment down the street from his dad's place so he could stay in close relationship? No. Jesus said, "And he went to a far country," as far away as he could get from his father's house. This was not a case of "I just can't talk to my dad. He won't listen to me." There was no desire for any further fellowship with the father. That was how Adam and Eve acted, though they could not have dreamed how different their lives would be without their contact with the Father. That's how it is with their descendants today.

Jesus doesn't tell us why the son took off for a distant country. I would like to speculate that the reason is similar to the reason college snowbirds flock to Florida, Texas, and California for spring break. I am not so naïve as to think it is just to lie on a sandy beach under a hot sun. Every college student in America who owns a motorcycle, and every high school student who has wheels or can bum a ride, heads for the playground. What happens? Normal, healthy, civilized, sane American young people come to Daytona Beach for a week and go nuts.

> "Well, because it's my senior year, and I've never been on spring break before and I figured, why not come to the place where it's supposedly wild and crazy and everybody goes. So we did."
>
> "This is the place to go. You leave everything behind. It's where you can cut loose."
>
> "A lot of people seem to follow other people. They change their ethics."
>
> "People, they like to come out here so they can party, get some sun, get away from their parents."

They start jumping off motel balconies and kill themselves when they miss the swimming pool below. They get so stoned they don't know where they are or who they are. They get sexually transmitted diseases. They get pregnant. They go nuts. Whatever morality they have at home remains at home.

Why?

LIFE IN THE MIDST OF CONTRADICTION

When you go to a far country, nobody knows you. Nobody's looking. You're anonymous. The rules of your parents' house don't apply if you don't want them to.

We wanted to learn more about the phenomenon of the far country, so guess where we went? The kids on the beach got the chance to look into a camera lens and talk about what was going on during their sunlit days and balmy nights when all the old moral barriers had been pulled out of their way. Did they think God in any way influenced their Daytona

Beach behavior? Their answers formed an interesting consensus:

> "Hey, whatever morality I got came from my parents. It's sort of been handed down in the family, and that's cool as long as Mom and Dad are around. But sooner or later I'm left to live a life without them. Then all bets are off. I can go somewhere else where I'm free of all that stuff."

That is the nice thing about a far country. There we're free. We can do whatever we want to do and nobody is going to tell our parents, nobody is going to tell our teachers, nobody is going to tell our ministers. Nobody is watching. Two young women I know provide a classic example. Stacey and Tracy are twins who grew up in a strictly moral home. Mom was fairly religious, and Dad went to church sometimes because he liked to have intellectual discussions with the Sunday school teacher, who taught about a Christianity in which one didn't worry much about things like whether Jesus was God or was raised from the dead. Christianity was a good moral code without such baggage.

Stacey met a nice hometown boy, eventually got married and settled down into a respectable life of children, church, and visits with grandparents. Staying in a small town environment, there never was much she could get away with because old lady so-and-so was looking over the back fence and she would have called Mom and Dad to report any suspicious activity. A reputation and family honor had to be maintained. Stacey wasn't one to rock the boat anyway, and when her husband was transferred to another city it wasn't long until her parents found a reason to move nearby.

Tracy seemed destined for a similar life. She, too, found a hometown honey and they set the date. But even as she got her final fitting for a gown, her husband-to-be died in a traffic accident. Their wedding day was the day of his funeral, and all the surface goodness of the family morality just wasn't enough to hold Tracy together. As soon as she could she headed for the most anonymous place she could imagine, Los Angeles, eventually getting a design degree and a liberated lifestyle. Like the prodigal son, she finally wandered home after several years in the city. She was sophisticated, disillusioned, and pregnant.

The twins represent the two contradictory ways of life—at home and in a far country. I can be one way on the surface when society is watching, but as soon as I get to a place where nobody knows me, I do what I truly want—whatever that is.

But the two lifestyles are definitely related. If all the person in the public arena wants is to "be good for the neighbors," the private life has no connection at all with the public one. Only the person who can openly show his or her true ethical self in public will feel like an authentic person rather than a contradictory fraud. No one's public and private moralities match perfectly. But they won't match at all without more of a foundation than home-grown surface morality can provide. Neither Stacey nor Tracy received a deep ethical base by which to live their true, private lives.

Does Daytona Beach anonymity, then, bring out the real you? For some high school and college students that would be a scary thought. Have you ever felt disgusted when you look in the mirror and see who is staring back? That disgust is a bit of self-honesty: "I'm leading two lives. I'm leading one life when I'm at home and another life when I'm in a far country."

There was a moment in my youth when I adjusted my ethics to face the contradiction between my values and my thoughts and behavior. When I was a little kid the whole world was at war. Hitler and Stalin were murdering millions of people, and the United States was engaged in a World War. My father was in Europe fighting, but at four or five years old, I couldn't understand why. The only thing I knew about my father was the ribbon hanging in the window in his honor, and the letters that came in the mail every now and then from the front. Every day the 5 o'clock news on the radio gave casualty statistics. I remember being terrified, wondering whether my dad had been killed and was one of those numbers. I asked my mother why Dad had to be away where he might be killed. Why did we have to live without him, and why were these people shooting each other? I would like to take care of this problem. I would like to go and talk to Churchill, to Hitler, to Stalin, and to Roosevelt.

"Could I please go talk to those guys and tell them that what they're doing is wrong, and it's silly, and it should stop?" I asked. At five years old I thought I had more brains than they did. Even though I was already a fallen son of Adam, I still had some vestige of ideals. I knew people shouldn't fight and kill each other. I knew people shouldn't hate each other. Children have a strong sense of fairness and justice, an innate ethic of what ought to be. But as fallen sons and daughters of Adam they apply that ethic to others more than to themselves. Hitler and Stalin should behave because my happiness was at stake.

Life got more complicated a few years later when I heard a three-letter word from one of the older kids in the neighborhood: S-E-X.

"What's that?"

This guy was more than happy to inform me, and he gave me a graphic description that shoved the whole story of the stork out of my life forever. He told me about how people behave sexually and the kinds of things they do.

I said, "I'll never do that. Why would anybody be interested in those sorts of things?" Then I went through puberty. . . .

All of a sudden I had feelings, attractions, enticements, and temptations I never had experienced before. Therefore, I turned the dial down on my ethics to accommodate my behavior. The contradiction of the thoughts versus the conscience was killing me.

I was a pagan; I had no relationship with God at all. Certainly, I wasn't a Christian. But even as a pagan I had a conscience. I knew the difference between right and wrong, and I knew I was leading two different, conflicting lives. And when I was away from my father's house, I operated on a different ethical basis.

DIRTY SHOES ON A WHITE CARPET

Why is the prodigal son called prodigal? He was wasteful. He was profligate. He sacrificed permanent happiness for momentary pleasure. Jesus said that he spent his substance on "riotous living." He was out of control. Riotous living looks like spring break at Daytona Beach. This guy had a spring break to beat all spring breaks. He spent himself on a spree of self-gratification, partying all night, then holding his head and retching all day. He was having a great time. Then the money ran out. He was oblivious to the fact that someday the bill was going to come due. He had absolutely no foresight, no wisdom. He wasted his money; worse, he was wasting his life. That's the word Jesus used: *waste*. I don't like people to waste my time or my resources. But, most important, I don't want anything to waste my life.

I was with one of the most famous business consultants in America, a fifty-five-year-old man who has been to the very top of the business world. He is a best-selling author. As we talked, he looked at me in deep sadness and said, "Okay, I've built the company, I've built the house, I've reached success. Now, all of a sudden I get up one morning and say, 'Now what?' There's got to be more." What he was saying was, "If there is not something more, then I have wasted my life. I've hit a dead end street, and I can't go back and take another road." Jesus said that the prodigal son blew it. He went from riches to rags. He became destitute. He had no money even to buy food to eat, and he couldn't get a job. Finally, he found employment, working in a pigsty. To appreciate what Jesus was telling his audience, remember that this is a Jewish story, told to Jewish people. And Jewish people are not allowed to have anything to do with pork. The pig is despised. They regard pork as unclean. When we read the story and say, "This guy has reached the bottom," Jewish people would say, "This guy has reached BOTTOM." He's a Jewish boy living with pigs and he's not even living with the pigs as a pig farmer. The farmer could at least sell some stock and buy a decent meal. This guy is living with the pigs as a pig. But he's not as big as the pigs. He's not as strong or as tough as the pigs. So he has to wait until the pigs have taken what they want, slobbering over the husks and dropping them in the mud. Only then can he get some of the scraps from the pigs in order to survive.

At this point Jesus' story has been about degradation. He has taken the son of a rich man from the pinnacle to the pit. I sure am glad he isn't talking about me. News flash! Jesus is talking about every human being who has ever lived on the face of the earth. We can see it in the lives of mass murderers and billionaire philanthropists, movie stars and starving, nameless masses in the third world. The description of fallen humanity is that we have abandoned the father's house and are wasting our substance and living with pigs. The honest description of fallen men and women is that we have taken life and turned it into a pigsty. It may be an air-conditioned pigsty, but it is still a pigsty. How can we possibly think of going home? Life in the presence of God must have been great, but the place where God dwells is all white carpet and snowy drapes. The scent of a clean breeze after a morning spring shower fills the air of his presence. And the truth is, if I may be candid: We stink, and our clothes are covered with manure. We even see ourselves as animals. Some of the students at Daytona Beach we questioned recognized this animal quality that means more than just a belief in the theory of evolution.

"I think we're basically all the same. Animals should have the same rights as humans."

"I think the basic difference between humans and animals is intellectual strata, aside from the biological differences, of course."

> "I'd say the average guy comes down here to party, basically, party."
>
> "There are no parents to give you ethics when you're at spring break, so you tend to make up your own, and at that age you don't really have any ethics."
>
> "The average guy is looking for a one-night stand."

Imagine going from the pigsty to the most fashionable and exclusive of dinner parties without taking a bath or even wiping your feet. That is the sort of thing nightmares are made of. The most dramatic and poignant narrative of any man's discovery of the purity and holiness of God is found in Isaiah 6. Isaiah was a prophet chosen by God to speak his message to the nation of Israel. The prophet had a vision of God's presence filling the great temple erected for worship in Jerusalem. Isaiah wrote that "I saw the Lord seated on a throne, high and exalted, and the train of his robe filled the temple." Above the throne he saw angels, who were calling out, "Holy, holy, holy is the Lord Almighty; the whole earth is full of his glory."

Now imagine you are in Isaiah's place. He sees himself standing in the temple, the holiest place in the world for Jews. But it was even more holy because the train of God's pure robe filled the temple sanctuary. There was no place to stand except on this perfection and purity. And Isaiah discovered that he couldn't even leave the temple to get away from the presence of God. The whole earth was covered with God's glory. Like it or not, God was everywhere. Isaiah couldn't escape. Isaiah was a man who knew God's fellowship as few have since the fall. But he didn't like being this close one bit, for he knew that he was living in a pigsty. The vision was devastating in its effulgent, brilliant, blinding display of the pure holiness of God. Isaiah fell on his face and pronounced a curse on himself. He said, "Woe to me! I am ruined! for I am a man of unclean lips, and I live among a people of unclean lips, and my eyes have seen the King, the Lord Almighty."

As soon as Isaiah was awakened to the character of God, he saw the vivid contrast between God's holiness and his own unholiness. "I have an unclean mouth," he said. "My mouth is dirty." He didn't know how dirty it was until he saw God. He didn't know he was in a pigsty until he saw the Father's mansion. But as he awoke to the character of God and realized his own sinfulness, he also knew that he was not alone. *All* people are unclean.

If misery loves company, so does sin. Paul tells us in the New Testament that the worst thing we can do is commit acts of disobedience against God encouraging our friends to join in our sin. Rebellion against God doesn't seem quite so dirty if we aren't the only ones doing it. Parents ask their child, "Why did you do what you did?" The child replies, "Well, it was Billy's idea." That deflects the guilt. The parents, who want to believe the best about their child, say the problem is that he is running around with the wrong crowd. Down the street Billy's parents are wringing their hands for the same reason. None of us admits that *we* are the wrong crowd. That's what Isaiah discovered: All of our mouths are unclean. We're all in this together. There's fellowship among pigs.

This fellowship is important to understand when we think about choosing our religion, if that religion is based on anything like absolute truth. The absolute truth is that every human stands unclean, and that is a serious problem if there is a clean, pure Being who is Creator of the heavens and the earth. We are an infestation of dirt on the good thing God made. That leaves two options.

First, if there is no absolute truth that helps us become clean in the presence of such a God, we are in a very bad way. There is no hope.

Second, if there is an absolute truth that makes us clean before God, this is very good news indeed. The good news is that we can leave the pigs and go home.

Jesus told the story of the prodigal son to let us know that the second option is the truth. Isaiah learned the same thing (see Isaiah 6:6–7). In his vision a burning coal was taken from the fire of purity and was placed on his dirty lips. He wasn't just cleaned by this coal. He was sanitized. His dirt was burned away so that it could not again infect him. He was told: "Your sin is atoned for."

How that happened is an important part of the story. The same Jesus who told that story of the prodigal son made the return home possible when he died on the cross to "atone" for our sins. The word "atone" has the idea of paying the price or satisfying the demand that sin be punished. We can split the English word apart and get a beautiful picture of what happens when the prodigal son returned home. The son was cut off from the father. When he returned they could again be "at-one" with each other. The son had become "dead" to the father. He was again alive to him and dead to the far country. He could not be alive to both. In his letter explaining what the death of Jesus means to the people in Rome, the Christian leader Paul said that the Christian's "old self was crucified with him so that the body of sin might be done away with, that we should no longer be slaves to sin—because anyone who has died has been freed from sin" (Romans 6:6–7). A little farther into his letter Paul declares this news even more powerfully:

> When you were slaves to sin, you were free from the control of righteousness. What benefit did you reap at that time from the things you are now ashamed of? Those things result in death! But now that you have been set free from sin and have become slaves to God, the benefit you reap leads to holiness, and the result is eternal life. For the wages of sin is death, but the gift of God is eternal life in Christ Jesus our Lord. (Romans 6:20–23)

Now think again about our friend in the Daytona Beach pigsty. You would think that this rich man's son would take one look around at the pigs and say, "I'm not living like a pig. I'm outta here. I'm going home." But he didn't, at least not at first. I think part of the problem is found in that word "slave." As bad as it is to be addicted to drugs, sex, or any other kind of pig filth, you know it will cost something to leave it behind. Perhaps it would be easier to stay in the mud and pretend it is a pleasant experience. What did it cost the young man? Certainly it cost any pretension that he was doing fine and didn't need anybody else. That can be a hard pill to swallow. I wonder how many of the students we put on camera in Daytona, who said that they thought their ethical life was just fine, thank you, were swallowing hard. What kinds of emotions and memories may have filtered through some minds as they proclaimed that their morality was at least as good as everyone else's?

Also, the young man may not have gone home because he didn't know enough about his father. He wasn't totally ignorant about his father. He knew enough about his father to know that there is no way in the world his father would approve of his behavior. This kid in the pigsty was scared to death of facing his father because he was frightened of the wrath of his father. And so he stayed away. He said, "I'd rather live with pigs, I'd rather eat with pigs, I'd rather waste my life than confront the wrath of my father." Because he knew just enough about his father to know that in some way the father was holy. And he knew that a holy father must disapprove of evil or he wouldn't really be a holy father. There would have to be a reckoning.

There was, as we shall learn. Jesus was telling my story, our story, the story of humankind. People can't wait to get away from the Father's house, can't put enough distance between themselves and the Father. They want to enjoy life their way, rather than the Father's way. So they end up in the pigsty but would prefer a pigsty to the facing up to God. That's us.

whistling in the dark

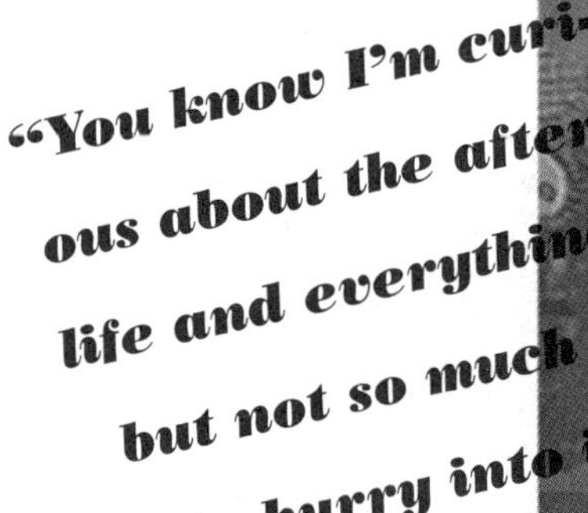

"You know I'm curious about the afterlife and everything, but not so much as to hurry into it."

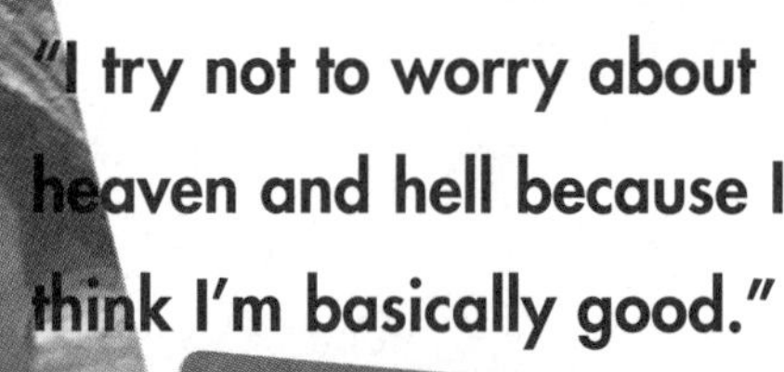

"I try not to worry about heaven and hell because I think I'm basically good."

"I really don't know if there is anything after life because it's never happened to me."

"If you play a real good role in life you'll definitely go to heaven, but if you don't you just wander. Your spirit will wander."

"I don't know if the question is if I *need* Jesus. It is if I, like, *want* Jesus in my life."

"When Christians talk about being saved I think they're dealing with the concept of salvation."

"I don't think looking into, you know, the afterlife and all that is really any of my business."

WE LIVE IN FEARFUL times. Recent generations of young adults in our society have not had as much reason to be afraid of dying as their ancestors. With vaccines and better medical treatment, relatively few children die of the diseases that once killed many. Except during wars, people coming out of high school and college statistically can expect to live a long natural life.

But I think the fear remains very real among today's young people, more than when their parents were young adults. Without a great deal of evidence to back up my gut feeling, I perceive that young people take death a lot more seriously, or are less naïve than were their parents about their mortality. Many high school and college students have stood by the casket of a classmate and friend. Drive-by shootings and traffic accidents are random, indiscriminate happenings. Child abuse, drugs, and suicide have made it more dangerous to be young. You probably know someone who has died of, or is now terminally ill with, a condition related to HIV infection.

CAUSE FOR FEAR

At the same time I don't see a whole lot of terror being expressed that after death one must face God. We run for cover from angry nature—hurricanes, floods, tornadoes, and earthquakes. But these dangers are inconsequential in comparison with the wrath of a God who has every reason to be angry. We would rather believe God has no reason for wrath and is a tame, grandfatherly sort. Haven't we just been talking about a father who is at the door waiting for the beloved lost son to come home? Now we will turn to look at the other side of God—a God from whom we need to be saved. We can't have absolute truth in our search for religion until we encounter a God who is creative and patient, loving and self-sacrificing, and infinitely angry with, and offended by, every person who stands before him as a sinner.

To ignore any side of God is to deceive ourselves. Humanity at the end of the twentieth century is afraid of the past, the future, the ozone layer, terrorism, nuclear holocaust, and AIDS, yet humans casually wander through the haunted woods of a far greater terror, blithely whistling in the dark.

We left the prodigal son with the pigs at the end of chapter 2, and gave only hints as to how the story came out. It's not much fun to stop a story in the middle, but that is where we must now search for truth in our religion. We have begun to build a structure, but it is far from finished and it looks a little strange. The house has blue bricks, pink window frames, yellow walls, and green doors. This imaginary house is only started. It is not finished. Unless we put more bricks on the walls, whatever its color, we won't be safe from the rain and cold. The house will remain unfinished. To finish the structure of religion we need to take into account the full picture of the God who is.

So far we have established the premise that there is such a thing as truth—a truth that agrees with reality. We have begun building on that premise as we looked at one aspect of that reality—humanity is in a predicament. I argued that Jesus told about the prodigal son, not to relate an isolated incident, but to tell a story about us. If so, then it is we who are now stuck in the mud of the pigsty. I don't know about you, but I want to get out of there. So did the prodigal son.

NEEDED: RESCUE

So why doesn't he just leave? He has options. His biggest problem is fear. He is afraid of dying of hunger, but he is more afraid of going home. He doesn't want to face his father's wrath. So, rather than face Dad, he stays with the pigs in misery. He is trapped, just as if the pigpen is surrounded by an electric fence and watched over by machine gun–toting guards perched in towers. Fear does that to you. Your brain turns to mush, and your muscles just won't respond. Steel workers who build skyscraper buildings see that fear at work. A workman walks the high girders for years, seemingly oblivious to the fact that death is a misstep away. Then one day, sometimes for no known reason, he will experience such terror that the muscles freeze in place. The person literally can die of fright unless rescued and brought to the ground. The body isn't the problem; the mind has been taken prisoner. People today sometimes freeze mentally because of the uncertainty of life on the job or walking through a dangerous neighborhood or facing fast-paced "future shock" change. Behind these fears lies a deeply embedded terror—a suppressed knowledge that a holy Father exists and is angry.

What has to happen for the fearful prodigal son to be rescued? In the plot line of a made-for-TV miniseries, this is where the hero is drowning, going under the water for the third time, and there seems to be absolutely no hope. We must tune in tomorrow night for the dramatic conclusion. We probably will, because salvation is at stake, and we want the hero to be saved. At its root, the word "salvation" means "rescue."

People mean a lot of very different things when they talk about being "saved." There is little wonder the student quoted above seems confused about what she has heard from Christians: "When Christians talk about being saved I think they're dealing with the concept of salvation." Well, I guess we are, but what are we dealing with when we deal with the concept of salvation? Christians can be obnoxious about it. Someone corners you in a hallway, grabs you by the shirt, gets in your face, and asks, "Are you saved?" I remember crossing the street on the campus of Temple University when a guy came up to me and asked, "Sir? Sir, are you saved?"

At least he said, "sir."

I had mixed feelings about the fellow. He was obviously a Christian who had a concern for me, and he was asking me a question so that he could give me the gospel. He cared enough to approach me like this on the street. At the same time, I wanted to ask him, "Saved from what?" Certainly I was not saved from strangers walking up to me in the street and interrupting me during my lunch hour to ask meaningless questions. One friend of mine was accosted by someone who shoved a finger into his chest and let him know in no uncertain tones that "Jesus is the answer."

"So what's the question?" he countered over his shoulder as he walked on. The guy was still standing on the sidewalk looking at him when he turned the corner. The unprepared witness to Jesus likely didn't have a clue how to respond.

Saved from *what*?

What is the question?

Are we who are Christians able only to spout platitudes about fuzzy spiritualities? Let's see if there are answers for the man in the pig pen who needs rescue from very real fear.

SAVED FROM WHAT?

The Bible speaks of salvation in more than one sense. Sometimes salvation refers to deliverance from an enemy—especially a superior army. When the people of Israel were leaving Egypt in the exodus, and the Egyptian army had nearly caught up with them to destroy them, Moses called out to them: "Do not be afraid. Stand firm and you will see the deliverance the Lord will bring you today. The Egyptians you see today you will never see again. The Lord will fight for you; you need only to be still" (Exodus 14:13). Read Exodus 14 and you will see that what happened next certainly comes under the category of dramatic salvation. Even Charlton Heston's version doesn't do the scene justice. Again and again when the armies of Israel went into battle against far superior enemies with more troops, better armor, and more chariots, and it looked as though the hosts of Israel were sure to be crushed, God brought the people victory rather than death, often through extraordinary means. The Jews would then celebrate that event as an experience of salvation. The song in Exodus 15 is a good example.

This kind of salvation did not mean that the souls of the people were on their way to heaven or that they were reconciled with God. Most of those people never showed much interest in God except when they were in trouble. But they were rescued from the calamity of military defeat. Years later Moses remembered these times of salvation and how the people had accepted rescue without turning to God. He said the nation was like a donkey that had grown fat with God's goodness and had "abandoned the God who made him, and rejected the Rock, his Savior." God had every right to be angry with people who had soaked up all the good things he had given them and then left him in search of a country far away from his presence. I wonder how many Israelites who had been saved and fed and cared for and then ignored God thought, "If I were to die tonight, and I was standing before God, and he asked me, 'Why would I let you into heaven?' I would say, 'Because I'm a nice guy.' "

Not a smart answer.

When Jesus was on earth and encountered sick people he took part in a second kind of "salvation." People would search him out because they had faith that he could make them well. Sometimes Jesus asked people to express faith that he could heal them, then say, "Go in peace, your faith has healed (or saved) you" (for example, Luke 18:35–43). Instantly these people became well. Did this mean that the people were saved from the judgment of God? Not necessarily, but they were saved from the ravages of disease.

WHAT IS THE QUESTION?

There is a third sense in which the Bible speaks about salvation, though, and this is what the man with the pigs needs. Someone might happen by the pigpen and give the man a large basket of food, or a $100 bill, or even a job. All these would be salvations of a sort, but they wouldn't be salvation from the ultimate calamity he really feared.

So what is this highest, ultimate salvation? At its most basic level we might compare this salvation to that of a boxer who is "saved by the bell." The fighter has taken some hard hits, but he is ahead in points. He looks like he's just about all in, and the challenger may be moving in for a knockout. Then the bell rings. The fighter was saved from defeat because the time ran out. He was rescued by the bell from calamity. It wasn't his own power that rescued him. By that power he wasn't doing so well. But something intervened.

Or someone.

Once a young Jewish couple was engaged to be married. But then the groom received some disturbing news. The girl he loved was pregnant—and he knew he could not be the father. Then he had a strange dream or vision, in which a messenger of God came to him with a three-part announcement: First, his sweetheart had not been unfaithful; in fact, the child conceived in her was a miraculous gift from God. Second, a son would be born to her. Third, he was to name that son Jesus, "because he will save his people from their sins." Jesus' name described his reason for becoming a human being. It is a Greek version of the Hebrew name Joshua. Among his friends and in his home Jesus was probably called Joshua or Yeshua. Translated into English the names all mean the same thing: "The Lord saves."

Jesus came so that the Lord *could* save from the ultimate calamity. What is the greatest catastrophe from which any human being can be rescued? It is the calamity that so frightened the young man who lived among pigs—the Father's just anger.

What sets off the Christian faith from all other religions? Why should you choose this religion over all other claims to ultimate truth? One imposing reason is the answer to two questions:

1. Who initiates my rescue?
2. From whom must I be rescued?

Of all religions that ever claimed your allegiance, only Christianity answers both questions with the same one-word response: *God.*

God is the Rescuer, the Author of salvation. If you have heard any statement from the Bible, there is a good chance you have heard the words of John 3:16: "God so loved the world that he gave his one and only Son, that whoever believes in him shall not perish but have eternal life." God, the Father in the story of the prodigal son, instigated, planned, and initiated salvation.

Now the second question: "salvation from *whom*?"

SAVED FROM WHOM?

God saves us from God. He initiates rescue from himself. Romans 5:9 says that the one who trusts Jesus for salvation is "saved from God's wrath." The Bible often makes it clear: Wrath is coming. Whose wrath? God's. God doesn't suggest. God doesn't threaten. God promises wrath. God announces in the Scriptures that he has appointed a day in which he is going to judge the whole world. And the New Testament calls it the day of his wrath. In Romans 1:24–32, Paul gives a frightening warning to people in the church at Rome. He tells them that God has already begun to judge humanity by letting them go their own way when they rejected him. Paul says that God gave them over to their own sinful desires and to their lusts. He gave them over to "a depraved mind" so that

> They have become filled with every kind of wickedness, evil, greed and depravity. They are full of envy, murder, strife, deceit and malice. They are gossips, slanderers, God-haters, insolent, arrogant and boastful; they invent ways of doing evil; they disobey their parents; they are senseless, faithless, heart-

> less, ruthless. Although they know God's righteous decree that those who so such things deserve death, they not only continue to do these very things but also approve of those who practice them. (Romans 1:29–32)

That could explain some things in the story of the prodigal son. This fellow thought he was heading for freedom to live the good life when he went to the far country. But when he tried to satiate his lusts he found no joy or satisfaction. Those lusts were, in effect, a beginning of the judgment for rejecting his father. The start of punishment for sin is more desire, more hunger, more dissatisfaction and lust to sin. And when lust runs its course and life becomes degraded, the pigpen in which we find ourselves is just the next step in experiencing God's anger. We were not made for such a life. It is unnatural and uncomfortable. We were made for fellowship with the Father, and we just don't feel good dwelling in the mud.

And yet Paul goes on to say that this is far from the end of God's anger: "Now we know that God's judgment against those who do such things is based on truth. . . . But because of your stubbornness and your unrepentant heart, you are storing up wrath against yourself for the day of God's wrath, when his righteous judgment will be revealed. God will give to each person according to what he has done" (Romans 2:2, 5–6). When you were a child you probably had a piggy bank. Each penny you placed in the slot did not amount to much. A nickel was not a whole lot to add to the bank. But you kept saving a little bit of change every day. The moment finally came when you were allowed to take a hammer and smash the bulging bank. You couldn't believe how much money you had collected.

A little bit at a time you had stored up a treasure. Paul says that is what people do. They invest in their account of unholiness every day and make themselves more and more and more despicable in God's eyes. Remember that he is holy and pure and cannot stand to be in the presence of evil. Ethical uncleanness is an infinite offense against his infinite goodness and cleanness. And during our time on the ultimate spring break we have been heaping it up.

And we honestly think God is going to just sit there and take it?

Deep inside we don't. That is why we are afraid to leave the pigsty and go home. But we keep it all below our conscious level. If there is anything the modern Western culture seems to be oblivious about, it is the idea of the wrath of God. There is probably no concept in theology more repugnant to modern people. Cases in point from our collection of student views:

> "That is not my interpretation of God, as a God of wrath. I think he is more forgiving or generous or kind."
>
> "You know God loves everyone, and he forgives everyone for their sins, so I can't say he gets mad at anyone."
>
> "Mad at me? Oh, hey, I've done some wild things. He probably could be mad at me."
>
> "Oh yeah, he's shown his anger. In fact, all through the Bible there's places that he's shown his anger at people. But, um, I mean I feel that overall he does that to show us, to show us his love."
>
> "An angry, wrathful God is not how I would like to perceive him."

"Supposedly God is all loving and all forgiving."

THE EXPERIENCE OF WRATH

If God is good, loving, and gracious, why should I worry about wrath? If God were really good he could never really exercise wrath, could he? Again, we have turned off our minds. We have forgotten what it means to be good. Paul told the Romans that God's judgment is based on truth—ultimate truth. Paul means that if God really is good, he has no option but wrath. A just, holy judge who winks at evil and refuses to punish it is not a just, holy judge. That sort of judge wouldn't be worth respecting. He wouldn't be consistent to the law or what he believed to be right. A judge without judgment would not be a real judge. That wouldn't be truth. Truth demands consistent holiness from a holy God.

There have been times in your life when you have experienced wrath. It is no fun when somebody gets ticked and punishes you. When you don't feel that wrath is justified it really makes you mad. But everybody at some point has experienced *just* wrath. You had it coming. If you deserve human anger and punishment, how much more do you deserve to be punished by an absolutely perfect, righteous, and holy God you have repeatedly, continuously, and callously disobeyed?

Why does he put up with it? You've insulted him, you've defied him, you've demeaned him. You've said, "God, I will not let you rule over me. I know better than you do." And then, after all that, we add, "Hey, no sweat. God grades on a curve. I don't have to worry. I don't do all the things that Charles Manson did. I'm not that bad. So why do I need to worry? Besides, God's mercy is infinite. He forgives everybody. God doesn't have any wrath."

Trust in that. You may be right—but only if the God who really exists is not holy. If God is holy, you had better expect wrath. You had better expect justice.

DEALING WITH REAL GUILT

That is the catastrophe we need to be rescued from. Paul says that in many ways, every day, God warns people that they are filling up the measure of his wrath (for example, Romans 11). In fact, the fear and discomfort of the muddy pigsty is not only God's punishment. It also is God's warning to prodigals who live with the pigs to come home so that final, eternal judgment will not come upon them. God is patient and kind and merciful and he waits for prodigals to wake up and repent. Peter, who had felt both Jesus' love and anger, when he was an old man spoke about the Lord's promise that he would someday return to earth in the last great "day of the Lord." Don't worry, Peter says, Christ will return. Be thankful that you have been given another day of opportunity to repent before he does: "The Lord is not slow in keeping his promise, as some understand slowness. He is patient with you, not wanting anyone to perish, but everyone to come to repentance" (2 Peter 3:9).

Of course, in our blind day God's patience is seen as a sign of weakness, or even proof that he does not exist. Because he hasn't done anything to you yet, you start believing that the hammer is never going to fall. But you can reach a point in your existence of saturating that measure of wrath. When that day comes, and you leave this life to stand naked in the presence of God, you're finished. For you, that is the day of the Lord.

You are without hope. God will abandon you and you will spend eternity in hell.

God is just and we are not. And, like the prodigal, we are in the pigsty. We are afraid of his wrath, so what do we do? How do we handle guilt?

I think most people handle guilt through denial. This practice starts when we are young. A child spills a glass of milk. Mom asks what happened, and he says, "My brother did it." Or, "It just fell." The two issues in guilt are accountability and responsibility. People are responsible to do what is right. When we do not do what is right we are accountable for our actions.

The man or woman who has rejected God rejects responsibility to God and accountability for thoughts and actions. Since God has put this accountability into our intellectual and psychological makeup, that isn't easy to do. In Romans 1, Paul explains this quite succinctly (verses 18–20). He says that humans suppress the truth by wickedness. Moving to a far country and wasting our substance in one orgy-filled spring break is a kind of denial that we owe anything to the Father. No one wants to feel guilty, yet we know inside that someone should be held accountable for evil done to another or to God. So we stomp our feet childishly and do the very thing that we know we shouldn't. It is a declaration of independence from God, as children declare independence from their parents when they are reaching toward adulthood. But there is a big difference. A time comes for all young things to break the ties of parent to child. We need no longer be dependent. But we are forever creatures of the Creator. There is no way to break that tie without breaking something significant in who we are. It ultimately can't be done without self-destruction. So we suppress. We partake of psychological denial that any of this has anything to do with us.

This is akin to the problem with crime today. No one wants to be accountable. Parents do not bother with their child care obligations. They reject accountability. Husbands drift away from their marriages and parenting responsibilities, for if things get bad enough the government will step in with AFDC payments. Mothers usually are left holding this parenting bag. But many mothers let their children raise themselves. This dynamic is hardly lost on the children, who never learn to accept accountability. Society owes them. They need not respect property rights or the persons who get in their way. With no sense of accountability they turn vicious and destructive. Their bodies fill morgues and prisons. We see the worst of this in the urban violence, but the problem of denial that leads to self-destruction is universal:

> "I've done a couple of things in life that I have been guilty about, but I try to put those behind me and not think about them and try not to do them again."

> "Well I try and live correctly, so I have no guilt. But if I feel guilty about something, then I do what's necessary to rectify it."

> "Sometimes I just talk about it, talk about why I feel bad, maybe to my friends. And they say, 'Oh don't worry about it, you meant to do the right thing. It's no big deal.'"

> "I guess there's no real way getting rid of that real guilt. If you've done something you've done something, and there's no way to go back and correct it."

"Sometimes my best friend and I talk about things, and that basically gets the guilt off my chest. Or if it continues I just try and cope with it until I feel better."

"I feel guilty sometimes about certain things that happen, you know, but you can't, you can't dwell on it. You know it's healthier to think about good things."

THE OPTION OF FORGIVENESS

There are two ways to deal with guilt. The first is to deny that it exists. We do everything in our power to deny our guilt or if we flat out can't deny it, we minimize it. And if we can't achieve that, then what do we do? We deny the wrath of God. We deny the justice of God. Many students we interviewed on the streets and on the beach at Daytona denied or minimized the wrath or justice of God. This is whistling in the dark.

According to the Bible and our own experience, this is not an effective way to deal with guilt. That leaves the second way. We must find a rescuer, someone able to satisfy God's demands for justice and payment for guilt on our behalf.

There is only one Rescuer for a human being who is unjust and unholy, but it is One we might never have expected. The God who held himself apart from defilement had to become defilement itself and pay the infinite debt for infinite rebellion. He had to take human unholiness onto himself and give to humans of his own holiness in order for them to become holy enough to know him. The problem was almost insoluble, for he could never, ever, ever negotiate away his own character. God will never stop being holy just to save us. But he could take on humanity and through humanity our unrighteousness.

Once sin entered the world, if anybody was to be redeemed, the cross was not an option. It was a moral necessity.

"I was taught that he died on the cross for my sins, but I don't really understand that. I never have been able to understand that."

"No, I don't know that there was any significance that Jesus was nailed on the cross."

"I don't know if Jesus has anything to do with being a Christian. I mean it has to have something to do with it."

"I do believe in God. When Christianity comes into play I get a little fuzzy."

"I really don't know what part Jesus plays in the Bible. I'd say he tries to, tries to help people. I don't know."

"I think all of us are going to heaven. No matter what we have done, no matter what the crime or whatever we've done, we're all going to heaven."

People don't understand forgiveness. They think that God simply waives the requirements and says, "I'll pardon you all." He cannot do that. It's not that he will not. He cannot—not without ceasing to be God. We think that he can be merciful by eliminating his justice. His mercy has to be a just and holy mercy. Justice must be satisfied. That is what the cross is all about, the satisfaction of the righteousness of God. But we have a generation of people who believe that you can be rescued from catastrophe without having satisfaction.

"I think it's important for people to have a faith if it helps them, but I personally don't need a faith."

"Right now I don't need Jesus."

> "I've known people who are morally upstanding, who don't lie, don't cheat, steal, etc. that don't go to church or don't believe in God."
>
> "No, I don't need Jesus, because I've got my own mind."

Some say, "Religion is fine for you, but you have to understand that *I don't need Jesus*." When I hear that I realize I am talking with someone who has fallen asleep to reality. I can understand that a person might say to me, "R. C., I don't want Jesus." But when they say, "R. C., I don't need Jesus," I ask, "Have you lost your mind? Do you hear what you're saying?"

If there's no God, of course you don't need Jesus. If there is a God, and he is holy and you are holy, you don't need Jesus. But if God is and God is holy, and you are not holy, there is nothing in this universe you need more desperately than Jesus. A holy God will never negotiate justice. His justice must be satisfied or he is no longer good. He is no longer just. He is no longer holy. He is no longer God.

There are only two ways that God's justice can be satisfied with respect to your sin. Either you satisfy it or Christ satisfies it. You can satisfy it by being banished from God's presence forever. Or you can accept the satisfaction that Jesus Christ has made. Jesus was God. God had to go to the cross himself to pay the price. That is why we use the word "redemption." The sinner must be purchased out of the pigsty. That is how God rescues people who are heaping up wrath. That is how God rescues people from his own wrath. The Bible says,

> Therefore, there is now no condemnation for those who are in Christ Jesus, because through Christ Jesus the law of the Spirit of life set me free from the law of sin and death. For

> what the law was powerless to do in that it was weakened by the sinful nature, God did by sending his own Son in the likeness of sinful man to be a sin offering. And so he condemned sin in sinful man, in order that the righteous requirements of the law might be fully met in us, who do not live according to the sinful nature but according to the Spirit. (Romans 8:1–4)

There is now no condemnation for those who leave the pigs and decide to go home by trusting in Jesus' sacrifice. You can embrace the satisfaction of the wrath of God that Christ has made on your behalf. The alternative is that you will surely face it yourself, on your own. That's the bad news. The New Testament does not invite you to Christ. There is no RSVP. This is a command. You are able to say no, but you are not allowed to say no. Refusal means everlasting damnation without a rescuer. The man in the pigsty couldn't get out until somebody paid the price.

This story has an ending. To that ending Jesus is pushing, because he loves the guy in the pigsty. What drove Jesus toward his fellow countrymen was to seek and to save the lost. He wasn't willing to let them stay lost, even when they didn't know they were lost.

You may be lost and don't know it. But God knows it. He knows where you are and there's no country far enough away that you can escape his presence. The most anonymous spring break reveler stands immediately under God's eye. You have kept a secret from your parents, from teachers, and from friends, but not from God. He knows where you are. He knows who you are. And he knows what you are.

He also knows how to change you, and he knows how to rescue you.

rude awakening

"Our purpose on earth? I really don't know."

"If there's a God when I die, there's, you know . . . whatever. I don't really hold strong religious beliefs. If there is one there is one. If there's not, it doesn't really affect my life that much."

"To be truthful, a lot of people don't like to get up on Sunday morning. It's simple as that."

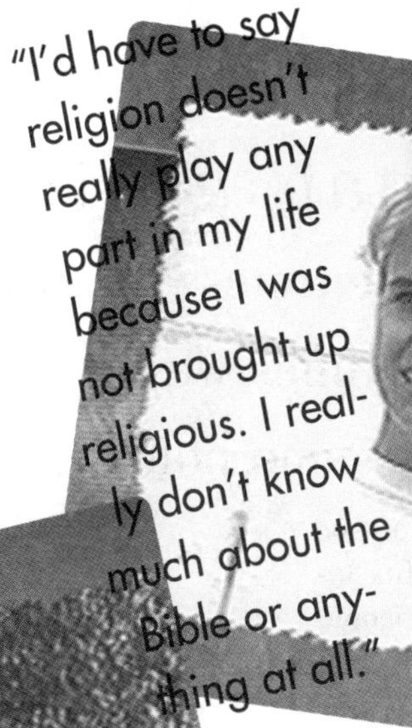

"I'd have to say religion doesn't really play any part in my life because I was not brought up religious. I really don't know much about the Bible or anything at all."

"I think the Bible is very interesting literature, but that's where it stops."

"The people who do claim to be Christian in some sense, many don't even believe in the Bible. Christianity is more of a social gathering for people now than it used to be."

IN CHAPTER 3 WE found that guilt can be deceptive. Sometimes we wallow in guilt feelings. Other times we deny accountability altogether. The same holds when it comes to forming our whole idea of God and how the universe fits together in him. Some people change religions with every book they read. But most people are unwilling to admit they have been wrong in the past—that the truth lies in a totally new way of thinking and living. Like the prodigal son, they are afraid to leave behind the old way of life. They need something drastic to get their attention. They need a rude awakening.

LIVELY CORPSES

When last we visited our friend the prodigal son he was still feeding the pigs and wishing he could eat as well as they did. He may know that he needs rescue, but he hasn't been rescued yet. He stays in the pigpen because he is afraid of his father's wrath. But every second he stays away from the father, more wrath is being treasured up. Wrath is increasing, so the idea of facing up to who he is has become all the more terrifying. The greater the wrath, the greater the fear. The greater the fear, the longer he stays away. The longer he stays away, the worse becomes the wrath. What a cycle! He will just not worry about it today. Pig life isn't so bad, given the alternative.

But one thing is happening behind the scenes that the prodigal doesn't know about. He wouldn't even care about this subplot while he is in a far country, morally and spiritually dead in the pigsty. Jesus doesn't tell us this part of the story. But it is there nonetheless. In fact, it is the punch line.

The Father knew what had happened in Daytona Beach, knew the boy was in deep trouble and couldn't come home. So he sent a Rescuer. More than that, he became the Rescuer himself. God sent Jesus—one part of his own essence—to satisfy justice. God made the only provision possible to restore this runaway child while remaining true to himself as a holy God. That dramatic rescue is the only reason the story doesn't end with the prodigal son wallowing in the mud with the pigs.

In chapter 1 I referred to my own experience of being awakened to the conscious reality of the presence of the Rescuer, Jesus, the Christ. I said that comprehension of Christ was the catalytic moment of my life, the turning point in the road when I finally completed the statement: "I believe . . ." Not long afterward I read the story of the prodigal son for the first time. I had no trouble understanding it. This was me. It was my story. But I wondered where Jesus was in it. Where was the rescue?

Oh, it is there, but as Jesus tells my story the awakening is dramatic and it also is quiet. It begins with the young man's stunning conclusion that he is really quite miserable there in the pigsty. Literally, what Jesus says (Luke 15:17) is that "he *came to himself*." Isn't that a funny way to say it? How does one come to himself or herself? I can come to Orlando from Pittsburgh, and I can come to Dallas from Orlando, but I can't come to myself spatially and geographically because I am always exactly where I am. Obviously, Jesus doesn't mean that there was a change in physical location. He is speaking figuratively, as we speak of a boxer who has been knocked out cold on the canvas, when the doctor jumps into the ring and uses smelling salts to revive the fighter so that he "comes to." The prodigal son *came to* after being unconscious.

Jesus actually was being generous in describing what happens when a person turns from guilt before God to forgiveness through Jesus' death. When the Bible talks about the human condition the metaphors most often used stress the individual's inability to do anything to change his or her miserable situation: *death*, *spiritual death*, or (at best) *bondage to sin and death*. The point being made is unmistakable. A person who has no life has no desire to change. The son who is dead could not care less about returning to the Father's house.

But people who are asleep or dead to God are seldom oblivious to their need for "something." Everybody in the world wants to be delivered, rescued, or saved from misery. This world is full of misery, disappointment, pain, violence, death, and disease. It's full of trouble. Everybody wants assurance that despair isn't the final word. I don't mean that everyone says they want assurance. The very point of much of modern art is that life is random and meaningless, and the courageous man or woman is the one who recognizes and faces life squarely at its most meaningless level. The celebrated, though interminable, play, "Waiting for Godot," puts this conception of life in the midst of unfulfilled hope before us. The actors are waiting for "Godot" (God), who obvious to the audience, is never going to come down the road. But the actors wait and talk, talk and wait, wasting time and their lives. But, perhaps without intending to, this drama establishes the fact that people are waiting and hoping. Hope is hard to avoid, even for existentialists. And the Christian view of the scene is that God has come down the road, but the actors have missed their rendezvous with him, because God didn't fit their preconceived image of him. They sleep the sleep of the dead.

WAKING THE DEAD

That sleep of the dead answers the great question of history: "Why, if there is a God, is there misery in this world?" The Bible says, for example, in Romans 5 and 8, that the cause of *all* human misery is sin. If there was no sin, there would be no misery. Herein lies the problem of the dead sleeper. All things—even hope of a better tomorrow—revolve around the desire for self-gratification. We want to be saved from our misery, but not from our sin. We want to sin without misery, just as the prodigal son wanted inheritance without the father. The foremost spiritual law of the physical universe is that this hope can never be realized. Sin always accompanies misery. There is no victimless crime, and all creation is subject to decay because of humanity's rebellion from God. The world suffers precisely because of human sin. Jesus shows this connection in the prodigal son's sojourn with the pigs. The son wants rescue from the pigs, but he doesn't want to go home to the father because he's dead in his sin. He's sound asleep to the holiness of God until he comes to.

That's what happened to me. Before I came back to God I went to church for years, but none of the news about rescue from the pigsty had ever gotten past my ears. I put up a blockade around my mind and emotions. Even then I understood that if ever I awakened to God my life would never be the same. I knew my life would no longer belong to me. That would mean change. So I'd go get drunk instead. I didn't want to listen to any of this—until I came to myself. And if it had been up to me I would still be in the pigpen. That is what being spiritually dead is all about. No one ever really comes to himself or herself without help.

Jesus once gave a life demonstration of what this is like (John 11).

Lazarus, a friend of Jesus became sick, and when Jesus delayed in coming to heal him, Lazarus died. As a matter of fact, by the time Jesus got to the home of his friend, Lazarus had been buried for four days. Lazarus's sisters, Mary and Martha, were heartbroken. If Jesus had come before Lazarus died something could have been done. Maybe if Jesus had gotten there at the time of death, he might have saved the day. But now the funeral was long-since past. So when Jesus ordered that the door be removed from the entrance to the tomb they strongly advised against it, for "by now he stinks." But they did remove the stone, and Jesus stood there and commanded Lazarus to come out of the tomb. And Lazarus came out, alive.

Nobody can suggest that a dead body that has moldered in the grave for four days just woke himself up. I was just as stinking dead before I came to myself. The only way you or I can be awakened from spiritual death is by the power of God. I have thought of that when hearing preachers say, "Step up here, come on forward, and be born again. You only have to make the decision."

That's like going to the cemetery and exhorting the corpses to decide to live again. The only way to come awake is for God to wake you up. The alarm clock God uses is his Word, the Bible. The Spirit of God moves in the hearts of people to awaken them and give them new life through the hearing of the Word. And so the prodigal son comes to. He awakens.

SIGNS OF LIFE

How do we know that the awakening was real? I've heard people say, "I'll make a profession of faith. I'll sign on the dotted line, I'll pray the prayer." And then, nothing. No

changed life. No sign of trust in God. It's like they just sort of turned over and zonked out again. They are no more awakened to the things of God than is a scarecrow. The evidence that a person has been awakened to God and has trusted in Jesus Christ for salvation is change. You have to get up out of the mud and start trudging toward home. It is amazing to see some of the things that people think amount to salvation in Jesus Christ. The following students have the right idea:

> "I think there is a difference between knowing God and knowing about God."

> "I think that it's important that you have that sanctity within yourself, that holiness or whatever. Like when you're a little kid and you could just go out every day and not worry about anything. You just felt cool, you know?"

> "I think man's purpose is, well, I think he was created to serve God and glorify him."

> "I believe that if you're a Christian you should behave differently than the people around you, because that's part of your testimony to other people, that they'll know that you're a Christian by the way you act."

> "I think that not only is it important that we believe in a correct doctrine, but we shouldn't just go around preaching the doctrine. It changes our lives."

> "When you change religions it's not like changing homes or changing your outfit or changing your hairstyle. It's a way of life and you have to

look at the entire world a different way."

One person was baptized as a baby. "No problem. I'm going to heaven."

Another person's parents were pillars of First Church. "No problem. My ticket is already punched."

Yet another walks forward at an evangelistic meeting, cries tears, prays the prayer, gets baptized, and signs the church role. "Man, I'm glad all that's over. I don't know what got into me, but at least I'm safe now."

One young man left behind his Roman Catholic parents to join an organized crime family in Chicago. One day his former parish priest ran into him on the street. "I've heard some things I don't want to believe," the priest said. "Some say you have even killed people. Do you know you have committed mortal sins against God?"

"Naw, don't worry 'bout me, padre," the man answered. "I got that all fated. I did seven first Friday Masses when I was a kid. Nothin' can touch me now."

At one extreme is the person who is on a roller coaster of emotion. Saved today, lost tomorrow. This person goes forward at every opportunity, but never gains any peace, and never really bothers to read the Bible much or make a change in behavior. At the other extreme is the one who knows all the right theology and says all the right things. This person may teach a Bible class or pastor the church. But the words just don't ring true to the bitter, selfish attitude, or the secret sins that are nurtured in the heart.

I've even known people who declared themselves to be Muslim

Christians. They were like the hapless farmer who wanted to stay neutral in the American Civil War. So he wore a blue coat and gray pants. Both sides started shooting at him.

There are a great many ways to "get saved," as many ways as there are people who are *doing* the saving. There is only one who can save, and that is the God who truly exists. There is only one place to go to for rescue, the cross of Jesus Christ. You are not redeemed by a profession of faith. You do not receive the benefits of Christ and the inheritance of the Father by a claim to faith, or by a decision for faith, but by the possession of faith. It must be real. The threat of God's judgment is real. The satisfaction of his justice by Christ is real. And the faith must be real.

How does one know salvation has truly come? If there are so many ways to get fooled, is there no hope of certainty that my faith is genuine? Imagine that you were walking downwind of the prodigal son as he walked that long road home. You could probably smell where he had been, but he obviously wasn't there any longer. The movement was obvious.

It isn't quite so obvious with someone who has faith in Christ. At first the changes may be subtle, and those around may still declare that you sometimes stink to heaven. Even if you clean up your act quickly and completely, though, others can't know for certain about your change. I can't know for sure about your faith. That isn't the important thing. The important thing is that you can. The proof is found in the story of the prodigal son. If anybody has ever had real faith, it was the prodigal son. How do I know that? He demonstrated it by leaving the pigpen—intellectually as well as physically. The first thing that happened to this guy after he woke up was that he said, "I will arise and go to my father." He knew a new desire, a change that utterly rejected the past and took another direction.

This was serious stuff, a catalytic turning point at which the man was saying to the world and to himself: "I used to believe happiness meant liberation from my father and self-gratification; now I believe this was all deception. I believe my life can only have meaning if I arise from the pigsty and go to my father." Emotion was surely involved in this decision, but it was not merely emotion. Intellect certainly came into play, but not merely intellect. Outward actions were involved, but the actions were not merely show. The actions indicated that a total turning of worldview had taken place, from one way of looking at life to another. When the son said, "I will arise and go to my father," in that moment he chose the direction his life must take from that point on.

THE LIFE AFTER NEW LIFE

There's a pernicious idea going through this land that a person can become a Christian without making this radical change. The reasoning goes something like this: I can accept Jesus as my Savior now, and I can accept him as Lord in control of my thoughts and actions later. Because Jesus died to release me from living under law, I have God's grace. He forgives all my sins no matter what. So it doesn't really matter how I live. I can accept Jesus as the Lord of my life, or not. It is a separate decision that has nothing to do with my salvation.

Perhaps you know someone who believes that. Perhaps you have believed it. Or perhaps you or someone you know has rejected Christianity because Christians behave no differently from anyone else. Whatever the case, there is not one person who truly has Jesus as Christ but does not turn over all of life to him now and forever. One type of relationship without the other is a non sequitur. It does not exist logically or in actuality.

Therefore, don't believe it. You cannot stay in the pigsty if you are a Christian. If you truly embrace the holiness of God and love and delight in the majesty of God you will be unwilling and unable not to change. You won't have it all together immediately, or ever. None of us lives without sin. But neither can anyone stay in the far country of open rebellion against God or the pigsty of moral death-sleep. If you rejoice in the satisfaction for God's wrath that Christ has performed for you on the cross, if God the Holy Spirit has made you alive, you will leave the pigpen.

The Gentle Jesus Syndrome

A couple of cases in point.

A woman is convinced that Christianity is all fuzzy feelings and being prayed over to get all her wishes. That seems to be the sum-total of her faith, and she practices it fervently beside her television set, listening to preachers who promise that God is primarily concerned with her health, wealth, and well-being, provided she sends for their latest book and calls their "prayer partners" with all her needs. Not all television preachers proclaim such a watered-down gospel, but some do, and this woman embraces each emotional ministry as one that is "truly anointed."

Recently she was observed watching (via television, of course) a recent dramatization of the life of Christ, one that stressed his humor and expressive love toward others. The actors did a wonderful job of portraying Jesus' humanity as they brought the words of the Bible to life, and she bubbled enthusiastically that someone was finally showing the real Jesus. Inevitably, however, the plot line wove its way through the meal in the upper room and the agonies in the Garden of Gethsemane as Jesus first experienced the full meaning of carrying our sins alone. A change slowly came over this viewer. She shifted uncomfortably and became quite agitated as the actor portraying Jesus stood bloodied before the Roman Pontius Pilate awaiting the pronouncement of condemnation.

"I don't think I can watch any more of this," she finally said, and hurriedly changed channels. The person watching with her said she turned away and clicked the channel selector, just as the first nail was being driven through flesh and the actor's eyes made horribly real the agony of crucifixion.

This woman's personal life and relationships with others are characterized by envy and bitterness. Yet she longs for and loves a gentle Jesus who hugs his disciples and caresses the brows of those he heals. Humor and gentle compassion are important aspects of the rabbi Jesus of Nazareth as he walked the dusty roads of Palestine. I am thankful that Jesus was such a teacher and friend. But the centrality of the Good News is not that Jesus laughed and loved, but that he was God become flesh, who paid the penalty my sins deserved by taking the wrath of the Father. It may not be pleasant, but the picture that is necessary for Christians to remember is the bloodied Christ who breaks our hearts because he took our place. This is the now-risen Lord of heaven and earth who now calls me to leave behind the pigpen and follow him.

What about this woman who wants a gentle Savior but not a crucified and risen Lord? Seeing only the fruits of her life and the superficiality of her desire for God, I fear that she will receive a rude awakening—now or later before a Judge who will not be laughing.

The "Carnal" Cop-Out

A pastor told me of his concern about a young man who attended meetings of the youth group. This guy habitually used drugs and was living with a girl. The pastor confronted the young man, asking him, "Don't you realize that this lifestyle is totally unacceptable to God?" The man answered, "What's the big deal? Everybody else is doing it."

The two came to an impasse. The pastor was saying that God's standard isn't what "everybody else is doing," that there are things God forbids. The young man was saying, "Hey, don't worry about it. I don't need to be obedient to God. I'm quite happy being a carnal (worldly) Christian. I'm Christian enough."

No, he's not Christian enough. He is not a Christian at all, and he too is in for a rude awakening, now or when he faces God. The prodigal son was awakened and resolved to leave the old life behind. He left the pigsty that day. He still smelled like pigs and he still had pig manure all over his clothes. You don't get rid of the stain of the pigs in five minutes. That's the struggle of the Christian life. Every now and then we still long for Daytona Beach freedom; we may take a quick tour through the pigpen. We can still mess up big time because we haven't gotten over our fascination with the pigs. But we can't take up residence with them and pretend to be Christians.

ACCEPTING AND BEING ACCEPTED

When he came to himself, the first thing the son did was file for a change of address. He knew about lordship, all right, and he knew he wasn't any good at being lord over his own affairs.

"I'm getting out of here. I have to go home.

"I'm not afraid of Dad's wrath anymore.

"Maybe there is a way to go home after all."

I'm sure the feeling of trepidation mounted as the son walked along the road toward home, rehearsing his speech. We can almost hear the wheels turning, even as the sweat pops out on his forehead, because the son knows that his father is perfectly within his rights to blast him out of the door with only a large shoeprint on his back side. He doesn't know about the work the Rescuer has done. His only hope, so far as he knows, is that an abject cry for mercy may cause his father to set aside the need for justice.

"I'm going to go home and I'm going to tell my father, 'I have sinned against you and against heaven.' "

Stop right there. I'm ready to walk into the pigsty and say, "Young man, I don't know what you've been doing hanging around these pigs, but you've learned some sound theology. You understand something that most people never come to realize." What the son had realized is that every time you sin against a fellow human being you also commit a sin against God. When I violate you, lie to you, lie about you, steal from you, or otherwise injure you, I also have committed a sin against heaven, because heaven commands me to love you, to honor you, to treat you honestly and justly, and not to inflict damage upon you. Remember King David, who took another man's wife and then had the man murdered to cover his tracks? He came to understand this point quite well, for his prayer of confession in Psalm 51 makes a bold statement in the first four verses:

> Have mercy on me, O God, according to your unfailing love; according to your great compassion blot out my transgressions. Wash away all my iniquity and cleanse me from my sin. For I know my transgressions, and my sin is always before me. Against you, you only, have I sinned and done what is evil in your sight, so that you are proved right when you speak and justified when you judge.

Whom had David injured in his sin? For starters there was the woman he brought into the palace for sex, possibly without asking her permission. That constitutes rape against Bathsheba. Then there was the murder of her husband, Uriah, a conspiracy that was carried out by David's general Joab, so Joab was also injured in a way. David committed adultery against his wives (for he already had more than his share of marital partners). Ultimately, he broke his vow of faithfulness to the nation itself, and Israel suffered many consequences because of this one sexual indiscretion.

After all that, David had the temerity, and the wisdom, to trace his sin to the ultimate of all offenses—sin against God.

Both David and the prodigal son had come a long way in understanding sin. No longer did they say, "Hey, I'm not hurting anybody. I'm just doing my own thing. Who cares if I choose to live with the pigs? Whom am I hurting?" Now they have awakened. Each says, "I have to go home. I have to go to my father, I have to tell him, 'I have sinned against you and against heaven.' "

So the prodigal goes home. What's in his head the closer he gets to home? His speech is prepared: "Father, I am not worthy to be called your son. Make me one of the slaves, but just let me be home. Just let me be in your house. Take away my status, I've already squandered my inheritance, I am not worthy to be called your son, but I want to be home so badly. I want to be in your presence so much that I'll take anything I can get. Make me a slave."

That is repentance. Compare that statement to the favorite call to repentance today: "Come to Jesus. Receive him. Accept him."

Accept Jesus? How arrogant. "Yes, Jesus, I accept you." Ha! Who are you to *accept* the Lord Jesus Christ, the King of kings?

The question on the son's mind was not whether he would condescend to accept his father. He wasn't that dumb. The person who asks you to receive Jesus isn't really that dumb, either. The problem is that none of us think as critically as we should about who God is when we say things like that. We have unintentionally adopted the "little God" view of our age. When going home to the Father, it is time to get rid of thought patterns born of rebellion. You are doing Jesus no favors by finding him acceptable. Anyone who accepts Jesus in the sense of, "Oh yeah, I'll take Jesus. I'll tolerate him," has not received Jesus. That person is still in the pigpen, spiritually and morally dead. David got past the biggest of all lies, the lie that God owes us a better life, or that God owes us rescue. Don't ever ask God for what he owes you; you might get it.

If he deals with you according to merit, you're finished.

So the son says, "Hey, make me a servant, just let me come home. I know I am no longer worthy to be called your son." No one is worthy to be called a child of God. No one is worthy to be called a Christian. I know I'm not. When you truly repent, as did David, you will say as David did in Psalm 51:16–17, "You do not delight in sacrifice, or I would bring it; you do not take pleasure in burnt offerings. The sacrifices of God are a broken spirit; a broken and contrite heart, O God, you will not despise."

Another writer summarized this true brokenness in the presence of the Father this way in Psalm 130:1–7:

> Out of the depths I cry to you,
> O LORD;
> O LORD, hear my voice. Let your
> ears be attentive
> to my cry for mercy.
> If you, O LORD, kept a
> record of sins,
> O LORD, who could stand?
> But with you there is forgive
> ness;
> therefore you are feared.
> I wait for the LORD, my soul
> waits,
> and in his word I put my
> hope.
> My soul waits for the LORD
> more than watchmen
> wait for the morning,
> more than watchmen
> wait for the morning.
> O Israel, put your hope in the
> LORD,
> for with the LORD is un-
> failing love
> and with him is full
> redemption.

Lord, don't treat me according to your justice, but deal with me according to your mercy, or I'm not going to make it. I know what I have earned. I know what I deserve.

THE HOMECOMING

Every step closer to his father's house, the prodigal son has to be worried that he will get what he deserves. But he did not know that every day since the Rescuer had finished his work, the father had been standing out on the porch, his eyes searching the horizon to see if any dust was rising from the road. The welcome mat was out, but the son was still missing. My heart is touched by the tragic pictures of little children one often sees in restaurants. Above the picture of each smiling child is the word, "Missing." What a parent must go through when a child disappears, never to be heard from again, must be almost indescribable heartbreak. It is always good news when a child is found and reunited with parents.

Such was the ending of Jesus' story. Off in the distance the father sees a cloud of dust on the road. He squints. He can't make out a face, but there's something unmistakable about the way this distant figure walks. The father's heart begins to pound. "Whoever is coming down the road walks like my son. Is it possible . . .?" Finally, forgetting all protocol, he sprints down the road screaming, "My son!" At last he knows for sure. He reaches the bedraggled boy, grabs him in his arms, and hugs him, saying, "You are home!"

All the while the son is crying and fighting to speak: "Father, I've sinned against you, I've sinned against heaven. I'm no longer worthy to be called your son, but I want to come home. Please, can I be your slave?"

"Oh, don't talk of slaves," answers the joyful father. "Come on, let's go into the house." Soon he is yelling out orders: "Go kill the fatted calf. Quick, give me the family ring. Call everyone to come feast with us, for we are going to have a feast. My son has come home."

That is the end of the story Jesus tells, except for one last character who arrives just in time for the festivities—the older brother. Jesus was looking straight into the eyes of the self-righteous, who figured they didn't need any Savior because they were raised in the church and never went through any nasty rebellion against God. They haven't been anywhere, and now they are ticked that the black sheep of the family is getting all of Dad's attention: "What? I didn't get the fatted calf. I didn't get the family ring, I'm still waiting for my family inheritance. He just went squandering everything, and you're throwing a party for him?"

In response to this charge, the father could say, "You fool. You are just as far away from me as this son ever was. The difference is that you are still in your death-sleep and can't see the ultimate truth of your situation."

Instead, Jesus focuses on God's joy at the arrival of any lost child: "This is my son, who was lost, but now is found." An invitation to all self-sufficient brothers was hidden in those words. Anyone can return home and be the guest of honor at a banquet. All it takes is to be awakened to the realities of the filth of the pigpen and the holiness and sacrifice of the Father.

asleep in the light

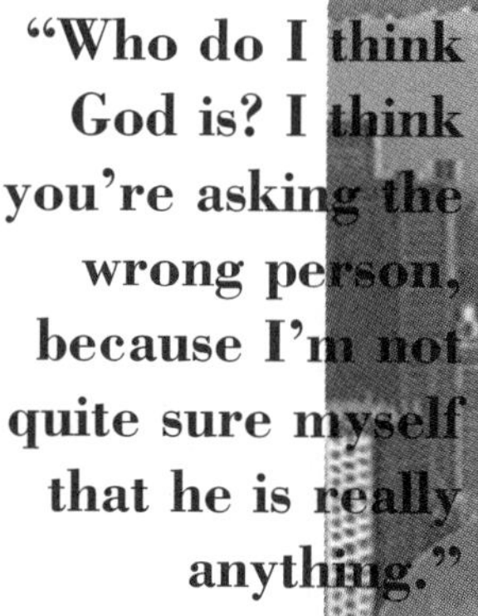

"Who do I think God is? I think you're asking the wrong person, because I'm not quite sure myself that he is really anything."

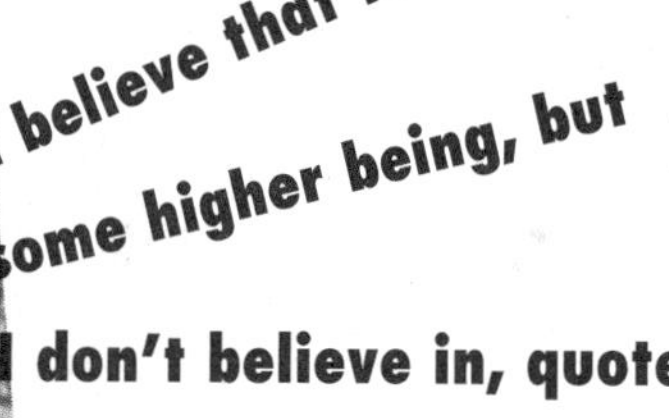

"I believe that there is some higher being, but I don't believe in, quote-unquote, 'God.' "

"Who do I think God is? I don't know, I think it's just a spiritual form."

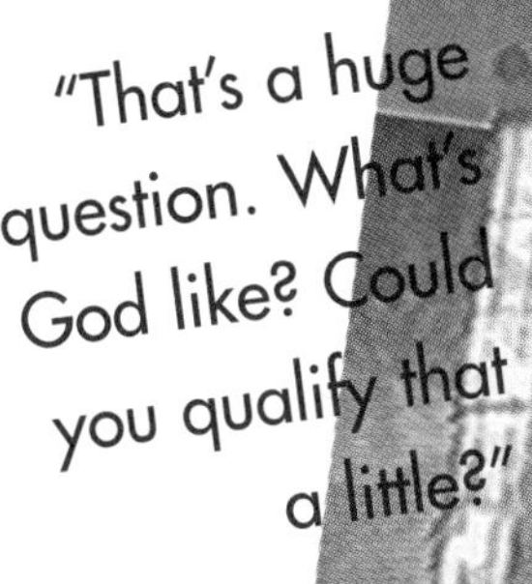

"That's a huge question. What's God like? Could you qualify that a little?"

"Really, no one really knows what God is really like. It's just that in the Bible it tells you how they picture him as being. Nobody really knows."

"I believe God is like an all supreme, all knowledgeable, omnipotent Being."

"I have faith that there's something out there, you know. I don't know what it is. I'm going to pursue it more. But right now I'm not sure about whether monotheism is right or whether we become one part of the universe or whatever. But heck, man, I'm only eighteen! I don't know."

SOMETIMES IT IS LESS important to have the right answers than to have the right questions. A man named Saul thought he did not need to ask any questions. He had all the answers.

The most important question, according to Saul, was "How can I be good enough for God?" He thought he had that answer down cold.

The only problem was, he was wrong. American humorist Will Rogers could have told Saul, "It's not what you don't know that will get you in trouble, but what you know for certain that just ain't so." Anyone who has followed the line of reasoning in this book should know that Saul's problem lay in the question "How can I be good enough?"

The answer, of course, is that he couldn't. But he didn't understand the holiness of God. No one who is separated from God understands his holiness. To tell you the truth, not many Christians do either. To complete our search to choose our religion, we need to be confronted once again by the ultimate truth of God. We must continually ask ourselves the right questions.

Saul had never asked the right questions. I think non-Christians often don't ask religious questions because down deep inside they have a sneaking suspicion of what the answers might be, and they don't like them. But Christians also are afraid of questions for the same reason, so they get into trouble. Or they are afraid other Christians will call them "doubters" if they are overheard asking the wrong question. They don't want to seem unspiritual or stupid. They also may be afraid God will lose patience with them.

But God loves to answer questions—the "stupider" the better—because he loves for us to have the ultimate truth we need to complete the sentence "I believe. . . ." He never loses patience with a question, and neither do people who are serving him. If you take a question to more mature Christians, those who really are men or women of God, you likely will find they don't think it is so dumb. Maybe they used to struggle with the same thing. Maybe they still do.

God tells us in James 1:5–8 that if anyone lacks wisdom "he should ask God, who gives generously to all without finding fault." James adds that what God doesn't want is for someone to ask with a waivering heart. The purpose of God's answer is to build a faith that is strong, single-minded, and founded on truth.

Saul's faith was strong and single-minded, but it was not founded on truth. He believed that he would please God most by persecuting the followers of that trouble-making rabbi, Jesus of Nazareth. It never occurred to him to ask a rather obvious question: "Who are you, Lord, and who is Jesus of Nazareth?"

So God had a question to ask this pompous religious leader. In order to ask Saul, God had to get the man's attention, so he tapped him on the shoulder (see Acts 9:1–9).

What he did was strike him blind. God knows how to get a person's *undivided* attention. Then he asked the question:

"Saul, Saul, why do you persecute me?"

Saul, with all the answers, didn't have a clue as to what God was talking about. Persecuting God? Wasn't he doing his best to serve God by ridding the world of the followers of a crucified criminal?

But now Saul did know what question to ask. He asked the most important of all questions: "Lord, who are you?"

That is when Saul started to become Paul the apostle—when he was confronted head-on by the holy God.

When it comes to evaluating a religion and choosing ultimate truth, "Who are you?" is the question God most wants to answer. Only after you see him for who he is can you have an intelligent belief.

ASLEEP IN THE THRONE ROOM

I have said here that to choose a religion that is true we have to know who we are. We have to see ourselves in Jesus' story of the prodigal son. It is more than an interesting story. It fits. It tells us the truth about ourselves.

Jesus did not intend for his story to only stir new self-awareness. The story brings us ultimately to the person of the father. Remember that he is the one who allowed the son to reject him and go his own way. He knew that his son was in trouble and he made it possible for the son to come home. He waited anxiously for his son's footsteps on the horizon. He declared a holiday when the repentant vagabond showed up at last.

Hidden in those character traits is the answer to Saul's question: "Who are you Lord?" Saul had plenty of theological education. He knew the Old Testament Scriptures, which revealed God. He knew the prophecies about the coming Messiah, signs fulfilled by Jesus of Nazareth. He and all other inhabitants of earth could see a lot about God by looking around at the world he created.

If we want to be really critical about Saul's question, it was dumb. He should have been able to answer it for himself. God had not shut him off from the light of truth. The problem was, he was lying asleep on the sand at Daytona Beach. Worse, he was spiritually brain-dead and feeding the pigs.

He was not alone.

The entire unbelieving world was there with him—asleep, though surrounded by light. But we Christians should not feel smug. Even we who have gone home to the Father and are bathed in the sun of the presence of God's Spirit in our lives occasionally drift off for a snooze.

To go to sleep in class can be embarrassing. To go to sleep spiritually in the throne room of God is idolatry. Idolatry means substituting a false God for the true God. A man who studied God's character throughout his life, A. W. Tozer, said it well: "An idol of the mind is as offensive to God as an idol of the hand."

And the same Jesus who described the father's delight in welcoming back the prodigal son was less delighted with Christians who had taken their minds off God and had gone to sleep spiritually: "I know your deeds, that you are neither cold nor hot. I wish you were either one or the other! So, because you are lukewarm—neither hot nor cold—I am about to spit you out of my mouth" (Revelation 3:15–16).

This sounds serious. I guess the search for ultimate truth doesn't end when a person answers the question, "I believe . . . " I also have to keep applying my religion to all of my life, so that I live awake, mentally alert in the presence of God.

SO WHO IS HE?

What have we learned about God, that we can stand awake in his presence? We know for certain:

1. God is powerful.
2. God is different from us.
3. God is pure and blameless—in a word, *holy*.

How do we know? For starters we can look around. If I want to know about an artist's mind I can begin by looking at the products of that mind. What media has the artist used? What subjects does the artist paint or sculpt? With what style does the artist paint or chisel or forge words? What does the work convey about beauty and truth?

> The heavens declare the
> glory of God;
> the skies proclaim the
> work of his hands.
> Day after day they pour forth
> speech;
> night after night they dis-
> play knowledge.
> There is no speech or lan-
> guage
> where their voice is not
> heard.
> Their voice goes out into all the
> earth,
> their words to the ends of the
> world. (Psalm 19:1–4a)

Isn't it ironic? What we need to know about God is answered every hour of every day in his world. What media did God use? Quarks and electrical charges we don't even understand choreograph the dance of electrons, protons, and neutrons of the elements. The elements spill out gases of suns and life-giving amino acids of the DNA spiral. God sculpted substanceless ideas into the laws of mathematics and logic. With brighter colors he painted the emotions of love and of spiritual life into the creatures he molded.

Everything that exists just happened? Are you nuts? Everything that is screams into our ears who God is.

But people move through creation like so many zombies. There is daylight all around, but they are asleep in the light—like so many sun-roasting hot dogs in the Daytona Beach sun.

Therefore, after sin came into the world, God did not depend on creation to tell about himself. He spoke directly through chosen people who wrote the Old Testament. Finally, at just the right time in his plan, he came himself to speak directly, the Rescuer, Jesus Christ. Jesus told us about God in words. He told us in the way he lived. He told us when he died for us on the cross (read John 1 and Hebrews 1). Look at what the Bible says about God, about Jesus, and about me. See if it doesn't provide the ultimate truth your life hungers for.

ULTIMATE TRUTH FOR SLEEPING SOULS

Before I became a Christian or read the Bible I knew that God was holy. I knew it every time I sinned and experienced a sense that what I was doing was wrong. I knew there was right and wrong and that a God exists who is rightness. I'm not talking here about guilt feelings. I'm talking about real guilt.

That's why I don't think too many people who have a firm hold on reality can technically be called atheists. Recently a man came to believe in God at a meeting of atheists. The speaker declared that he was going to give God three minutes to prove himself by striking him dead. The man stopped speaking and stared at the clock on the wall. In perfect silence one minute passed, then two, and at last three. As the deadline passed there was an audible exhalation of air throughout the room. People had been holding their breath.

"I knew in that moment that we were a bunch of hypocrites. There wasn't a real atheist in the place," the man said.

So, if there is a holy God, what do I do with my guilt? That's what the story of the prodigal son is all about.

I've experienced that in my life; I know what it means to come back from the pigpen. I know what it means to fall on my face before God. I know what it means to have God reach down and put his arms around me like the father did the son. I have felt the robe put around me, and the ring of identity put on my finger. I've been brought into the banquet feast of fellowship.

What I want more than anything else is that you have that same experience. When we do sin before a holy God who really exists, we really do stand naked in his presence. We really need to be covered. We need the cross, because God will never negotiate his holiness. He loves to be holy, and he hates everything that isn't holy. Only because Jesus took our unholiness onto himself and gave us his own holiness could we be covered.

A great many people talk about the redemptive power of the cross as an abstract symbol or a pattern for selflessness. We can be spectators of the cross in the abstract. Abstract crosses do not take away my guilt. Something personal has to relate me to a moment in space and time history when nails were driven through the flesh of Jesus. In that execution an infinite God paid an infinite penalty for my infinite rebellion.

Those same people talk nebulously about *faith*. What I mean by faith is that we personally trust in Christ to cover us. Christ alone can bring us back into fellowship with the God who is holy. He supplies what we need. I'm not righteous, and you're not righteous, but Christ is perfect righteousness. And he has traded our rebellion for his own righteousness if we will accept him as Savior and Redeemer.

That's a major step in anybody's life. I think it is the most significant decision a person ever makes. Guilt can be settled between you and God right now. It is settled by coming to the cross. Jesus is called Savior because he can save you from nakedness before God and his wrath. He is called Redeemer because he paid the infinite penalty you owed but could never pay.

Of all the religions and philosophies in the world, only one offers Jesus Christ. Only one promises the great banquet feast with the Father, with signet rings for his sons and daughters.

ALIVE TO GOD OR BRAIN-DEAD?

Unfortunately, I have a great enemy who stands in the way of my enjoying the promised presence of God: me. I used to be asleep to the light of God as an unbeliever. But I am still caught napping in that light, mentally and spiritually.

It started while I was a college student, just after that catalytic moment when I came to know Jesus as Savior and Redeemer. I have to confess that one of the immediate results of my conversion was that for the first year of my Christian life I was almost brain-dead. I fell in love with Jesus. The only thing I wanted to know anything about was Jesus. So what's wrong about that?

What's wrong is that Jesus doesn't want to be the end of a Christian's thinking. He wants to be the center.

I was a freshman in college, and my professors had ideas about what I should be learning. I wasn't interested in anything so unspiritual as what they wanted to teach me. My feeling was, "I don't care about biology. I don't care about sociology. I don't care about psychology. All I want to know is Jesus."

So I read the Bible. That's just about all I read that year, except for some books about the Bible. You can imagine what my grades were like. I got an "A" in gym because I was on a football scholarship, and I could ace gym without even showing up for class. But it was only a one-credit-hour course, and each credit was worth three points if you got an "A." I also got an "A" in Bible, which was a two-credit course.

All the rest of the grades were "D," which gave no points at all. At this college if you only had two points at the end of the first semester, you were history. I had three and made the "dean's list"—the dean's probation list. The next semester I did no better. That semester I went through my "evangelist phase." All I wanted to do was to talk to people about Jesus. I wanted to be an evangelist. I told all my friends about what had happened to me. They thought I had lost it. I wanted to tell the world I had experienced something unlike any other experience of my life. But I still was completely hostile to any education other than the Bible.

Then I had my second catalytic experience.

The college required that I take a certain number of courses in lab science, a certain number in non-lab science, and a certain number in the social sciences. For one of these last requirements I enrolled in Introduction to Philosophy.

Talk about dry.

For my first assignment I read David Hume's *Inquiry into Human Understanding*. Which human's understanding this guy was inquiring into, I had no idea. Next we read something by Immanual Kant, and I was even more confused. To make matters worse, the professor was soft-spoken in class and his teaching style lacked passion. Frankly, he was boring. I went to the class every other day, and when I was present my mind remained absent. It wasn't as if I was wasting the time: I tuned out the lecture and read pamphlets of sermons by Billy Graham. I was reading about Jesus, and that's all I wanted to know. I hid in the back of the room and propped up my notebook so the teacher wouldn't see that I was ignoring him. My soul was awake to God, but my mind was asleep.

All this changed the afternoon the professor lectured on the philosophy of Augustine. He explained this early Christian theologian's philosophical understanding of creation. I perked up my ears. I wasn't so committed as to pick up my pen to take notes, but I did close Billy. That soft voice explained Augustine's view of the majesty manifested in a Being who could bring a universe into existence by the sheer force of his command. Augustine was blown away at a God so transcendently powerful that he could simply say, "Let there be light," and the lights came on.

I was blown away with him. My mind came awake. I had to learn more about this God who is so powerful, great, and majestic.

Being an impulsive person, after that class I went directly to the registrar's office and changed my major from Bible to philosophy. It was not that I wanted to study philosophy so badly; I was still brain-dead as far as Kant was concerned. But I wanted to study under that teacher. God used that man to awaken me to a new understanding.

TOUCHING THE DIVINE

If you are covered by Jesus, your life is to be defined by a pursuit of the knowledge of God. The work just starts when you're converted. It was Jesus who said, "Seek first his kingdom and his righteousness, and all these things will be added to you" (Matthew 6:33). If the first question you should ask is how to finish the sentence, "I believe . . . ," there is a second question: "Do I have an intense, vivid, powerful sense of the presence of God?"

I ask that question of others quite often. Most people don't even hesitate to say, "Yes, I've had it. I've had rare moments in which the presence of God was so powerful, so real, that I could touch the divine."

My next question is more provocative: "What happened?"

This is a trick question. When I first started asking this I really meant, "What was it like? What did you sense? What were your thoughts?" But no one interprets it that way. They think I mean, "What happened that you haven't continued to feel God's presence like that?"

I certainly have not sensed the presence of God vividly every minute of my life or every day of my life since I was awakened to the majesty of God. I admit it—I still mentally prop up my book in front of me in class. I must continually be awakened to the character and holiness of God. But when I wake up I feel foolish, because I've been missing so much. If you have sensed the close presence of God, think what it was like. Some people say, "It was eerie" or "It was scary" or "It was dreadful, awful." But I doubt you will say, "It was boring."

Yet lots of people tell me that being in church is boring. If God isn't boring and church is boring, I can only figure that, for some reason, we're not meeting God there. That's not a good sign, because church is where we join other Christians with the express purpose of meeting God. God's there, I'm there. But we don't connect. I don't touch him. I don't sense him because I'm asleep.

Some people say, "Yeah, I know the experience, and it's wonderful. I feel a sense of calmness or peace flooding over me." However we describe it, the one thing we know is that it is very different from normal human experience. Why is it different? God is different. He is so high, so great, so transcendent, so beautiful, so majestic so unlike anything in this world. And yet the prodigal son who has come home is invited to touch this reality of the spiritual dimension of life. God didn't create us to be foreign to this reality. Adam and Eve must have felt at home in it before sin built its great wall between people and God. Yet the normal Christian desires to experience it fully. It is one of God's greatest gifts to us while we live on earth. Isaiah 57:15 describes this gift from God's perspective: "For this is what the high and lofty One says—he who lives forever, whose name is holy: I live in a high and holy place, but also with him who is contrite and lowly in spirit, to revive the spirit of the lowly and to revive the heart of the contrite."

Who can we describe as lowly and contrite? Certainly that was the attitude of the prodigal son when he had come home. He had lost all pretensions about being anything special. Isaiah gives the contrite a great promise: We will be revived. Our hearts will be strengthened, cared for, and nourished, so that we will grow more awake spiritually. That is a great goal for every Christian life—to stay awake so God will revive us and help us stay awake to knowing him as he is.

GREAT, GOOD, AND HOLY

I remember the first prayer I ever learned; I wasn't a believer, but I was raised in a religious family, and we had table grace at every meal. My grandmother, who lived with us, made me memorize a prayer I had to say every night. The dining room table would be set and we would be seated. Then I got my cue: "Okay, Sonny, say the prayer."

> "God is great,
> God is good,
> And we thank him for this food."

That was my introduction to prayer and to theology, which wasn't a bad beginning. That prayer taught me two things about God. First, God is *great*; second, God is *good*. Years later, when I was studying theology for real, I spent a lot of time trying to understand a third descriptive word about God. God is *holy*. I've used that word in this book, though you do not fully understand what it means. No human fully understands what it means as it describes the greatness and goodness of God. God's holiness stands behind everything else we can say in describing God. As holy,

1. God is totally separate and above everything else. We sometimes use the word "transcendent" to describe this separateness.
2. Awe and fear are the proper responses to God, fear in the sense of standing in the presence of something of limitless power and magnificent majesty.
3. God is absolute moral and ethical perfection.

The most basic characteristic that defines God is his holiness. Angels sing in his presence, "Holy, holy, holy" (Isaiah 6:3 and Revelation 4:8). When Jesus taught his disciples to pray, he first taught them to pray about God's holiness: "Our Father in heaven, hallowed be your name." People mumble through this prayer hundreds of times without thinking what it means. That is ironic because the prayer is talking about people who are sleeping through life without a thought of God's holiness. Jesus is saying to the disciples, "I want you to pray that the Father's name will be regarded as holy. I want people to *wake up* to who my Father is! I want people to understand that he is holy, and that he will never negotiate his holiness."

God will never stop being holy. He loves to be holy and he hates everything that isn't holy. People who are asleep have no regard, no reverence, no worship, no adoration, no praise for his holiness. Instead, they hold his holiness in contempt. They use his name to curse. They say, "God isn't holy. He forgives everybody without repentance, without satisfaction, without atonement. I don't need Jesus." That reminds us of some of the responses to our informal video poll of students, who said such things as:

> "I haven't decided I don't want to have anything to do with Christianity. It's just that right now I have no time, I really don't have the interest to get into it. I may one day. One day I may decide that I want to be religious, you know. There is a God, but right now in my life I really don't believe the Bible."

"I think Jesus was a mental healer, a feel-good kind of guy, who smiled, waved, and made you feel good."

"God lets you slide by."

"God doesn't have any wrath. He's kind and loving."

If you want to divide people in a hurry, focus on the holiness of God, because nobody's neutral about it. Just ask yourself, "How do I really feel about the holiness of God?" If you don't delight in the fact that your Father is holy, holy, holy, then you are spiritually dead. You may be in a church. You may go to a Christian school. But if there is no delight in your soul for the holiness of God, you don't know God. You don't love God. You're out of touch with God. You're asleep to his character.

How can I say something so narrow and absolute? Think back over the content of this book and to the meaning of holiness—God's awesome, transcendent, majestic power and being, and absolute purity. The only reason we *can* delight in God at all is because he is holy in greatness and goodness. Imagine a God who is

- the highest being in the universe
- all-powerful
- all-knowing; able to know every detail of your life and thoughts
- always present
- infinite
- eternal
- unchanging
- not good

Life in a universe ruled by an all-powerful, all-evil God would be unbearable. Our only hope is that this universe is governed by an all-powerful, all-holy God who will never ever use his power and knowledge in an unholy way. God is great and he is *good.*

THE BOTTOM LINE—HOLINESS AND SIN

I remember one of my early experiences as a teacher. I figured I would have no trouble with a group of high school kids in the church. I loved high school kids. I wasn't far removed from being one myself. I figured I would never forget what it was like to be a teenager. "I'll always remember. I'll always be able to relate," I said with self-congratulation.

I began by announcing the subject of discussion: "Why you hate God."

I walked out of that class saying that I'd never talk to high school kids again as long as I lived.

They got so mad when I suggested that their basic human nature was hostile toward God. They insisted that they were never, ever hostile toward God. They were hostile toward me, they said, but they weren't hostile toward God. However, the Bible says something different. The Bible says that our fall is so great, our corruption so profound, that we don't want to think about God. And the very thing that makes God so loathsome to us is his holiness.

Through a lot of the quotations of college students in this book, I hope you have noticed something. Few of them had anything really nasty to say about God. They may not think there is a God, but if there is, hey, that's cool. But few felt a lot of awe about God's greatness or goodness. They don't feel they hate God; they are just indifferent toward him. That is the hallmark of a culture where all truth is relative. It seems safe to be indifferent. The "fanatics" are the ones who don't fit.

But how does a God who is holy in greatness and goodness regard indifference? It is contempt for his very being. It is much like the contempt the son felt for his father when he asked for his inheritance in Jesus' story. That son would probably have denied that he hated his father. But his actions showed that he did.

If you are searching for truth today, the ultimate truth you can use to complete the sentence, "I believe . . ." you will have to move against the flow of human nature. You will especially have to move beyond the limits of relative truth in our society. By the time they had reached high school, those students in my class had already stripped God of his holiness, his justice, and his wrath. They had conjured up a God who is only love, kindness, mercy, and grace. He is a cosmic bellhop who would follow on command. They preferred a God who never sends anybody to hell, never makes absolute demands on our lives, and is ready to forgive any infraction.

Who would hate a God like that?

But the unhated God is a substitute, an idol traded for the real God. People hate the real God so much that they set up their own versions to replace him. Make no mistake. Your basic nature is to hate the God who made you. Even conversion doesn't get rid of that altogether. You are an idol factory. Christians run from the holiness of God. Christians run from the sovereignty of God. They don't want a God who is sovereign, except when they need something. This is because the greatest enemy of sin is holiness.

The prodigal son understood that. We understand that. We understand that, if God is holy, we are in trouble. We are not holy. That's why we push God out of our minds. Two things we don't like to think about: his holiness and our sin.

But if you want life, you must face both of them. And when you do face his holiness and your sin they will lead you home to the Father's door, smelling of pig but rescued from death and forgiven.

At the end of the road home prodigals will be revived if they find the only experience that gives life meaning—knowing the presence of God.

Dr. R. C. Sproul, theologian, minister, and teacher, is chairman of the board for Ligonier Ministries. He is widely known for his videocassette series on such topics as character, the Christian worldview, and God's holiness. His many books include *Surprised by Suffering, Pleasing God, Chosen by God, One Holy Passion, Not a Chance,* and *Faith Alone.*